INDELIBLY DAVIS

INDELIBLY DAVIS
A Quarter-Century of UC Davis Stories...and Backstories

LARRY N. VANDERHOEF

ISBN 978-0-9863701-0-6 (hardback)

Digital book available, with video extras, at:

http://escholarship.org/uc/ucdavischancelloremeritus_books

Project Management: Maril Revette Stratton and Cynthia Geronimo Contreras

Design: Jan Conroy and Laurie Lewis

Editing: Maril Revette Stratton

Photography: Debbie Aldridge, Michael Brooks, Renée C. Byer, Sue Cockrell, Kathy Keatley Garvey, Tia Gemmell, Todd Hammond, Karin Higgins, D. Kern Holoman, Enrique Lavernia, Florence Low, Stephen McKone, Tom McNeill, Neil Michel (Axiom/Neil Michel Photographs, AR-195, Special Collections, University of California Library, Davis), Ellen Pontac, Denis Poroy, Allison Portello, Joe Proudman, Cheng Saechao, Maril Stratton, Wayne Tilcock, Gregory Urquiaga, Larry Vanderhoef, Jim von Rummelhoff, Corey Yeaton.

Illustrations: Scott Ahrens (p. 143), Jan Conroy (p. 12)

Videography: William Breidenbach, Jeremy Cooke, Robert Craig, Mark Holman, Alan Jackman, Bill Lorfing, Kris Naegeli, Paul Pfotenhauer, Chris Stone, Christopher Terry, Kit Tyler, Paul Ver Wey, Ken Zukin

Printed by CDS Publications, Medford, Oregon. Print production management by UC Davis Repro Graphics.

TO MY MOTHER, Ida Lucille Wothe Vanderhoef, who lived by guiding principles, believed in the goodness of hard work, kept promises and trusted in the life-changing opportunities only a good education can provide.

AND TO MY WIFE, Rosalie Slifka Vanderhoef, my best friend and lifelong partner, with love and gratitude.

CONTENTS

Preface

Books by former university administrators aren't likely to sail off library shelves or tally an impressive number of digital downloads.

But I hope this book—a telling of select stories (and backstories) across 25 pivotal years at the University of California, Davis (arguably the period of its greatest physical and academic growth)—will appeal to members of our campus family curious to know more about the unique path that has led to who we are today.

I learned long ago as provost (1984-1994) and chancellor (1994-2009) the importance of hearing and sharing UC Davis' many stories, of understanding and appreciating the campus's history and distinctive culture. Those stories reveal what we value, how we behave (in good times and in bad) and how we optimally set our sails for changing winds. They helped me lead.

This book aims to round out our UC Davis anthology with stories that will tell you something new (and special) about the campus, that are relevant to its development and identity, and that touch on its values and culture—on that special spirit that revered former UC President Clark Kerr believed set it apart from all other UC campuses.

These stories are my memories, augmented by corroborating research and interviews.

I've done my best to write accurately and fairly and with clarity and candor (and, at times, with entirely appropriate chagrin) about topics that, across the years, have stayed strong on my mind. Stories about people who radiate that special Davis spirit…about wished-for do-overs…about conflicts (and responses)…about heartbreaking tragedy… about wing-and-a-prayer risk-taking…about the payoffs of patience and persistence… and about tough, principled decision-making (what my dad would call "having starch").

And I've tried to add to the record—and, in some cases, to correct it. I've tried to tell the story behind the story, to tell you something you likely don't already know.

Of course, the story-telling is incomplete—really just a sliver. But I hope these stories, gleaned from my quarter-century on the 5th floor of Mrak Hall, will add to the rich narrative of a university with a remarkable past and even brighter future.

Serving as UC Davis' chancellor was the honor of a lifetime. As I said at my inauguration and say again today, thank you so much for having me.

▶ **http://escholarship.org/uc/ucdavischancelloremeritus_books**

AAU's Belated Invitation

No guile, no strategy, no nothin'.
—FORMER PROVOST AND
    EXECUTIVE VICE CHANCELLOR ROBERT GREY

WHO KNEW?

Well, apparently Henry Yang, chancellor of UC Santa Barbara. But, unfortunately, not Bob Grey and I.

Steve Sample, president of the University of Southern California, was coming to chat with us—and, we understood, with a few other UC chancellors and provosts—that early spring of 1995.

UC President Jack Peltason had recently announced his intention to step down, and the scuttlebutt was that Sample was potentially interested in replacing him. Our meeting, we surmised, was part of his UC research.

That Steve's visit might be related to the Association of American Universities—whose exclusive membership invitation is coveted by North American research universities—never crossed our minds.

I suspect most everybody can identify a particularly memorable screw-up in their careers. This definitely was ours.

Thinking we were helping Steve decide whether he wanted to be UC's next president, for nearly two hours Bob and I answered with utter honesty his every question about the campus's breadth and quality. We readily described UC Davis' strengths and weaknesses, with no intention at all to "sell"

Steve Sample, former president of the University of Southern California (Photo: USC)

the total institution. We knew the campus's achievements and shortfalls, and we were forthright in describing them—in retrospect, painfully so. After all, we thought, Steve Sample needed an accurate assessment if he were to be UC's next leader.

We knew Steve's reputation as an excellent university administrator. He'd masterminded USC's turnaround from what one UC San Diego professor had once described as "a core of athletics surrounded by a veneer of academics" to one of the nation's most respected research institutions. He'd carved out major amounts of undergraduate scholarship money for recruiting National Merit Scholarship winners. He'd insisted that university departments hire only the best faculty—National Academy members, winners of prestigious national and international prizes, scholars with impressive numbers of publication citations. He'd championed innovative community partnerships that had won national acclaim—and given UCLA a run for its money as Southern California's "true" land-grant university. And he was a prodigious fundraiser, helping to amass nearly $3 billion for USC—completing, at that time, the second most successful fundraising campaign in the history of higher education.

And before USC, he'd similarly helped The State University of New York at Buffalo leapfrog to greater academic accomplishment and prominence—all the way to the AAU, against very tall odds. That coveted membership invitation came in 1989, seven years after he'd become SUNY-Buffalo's president.

Steve Sample was not one to leave his goals to chance. He knew how *U.S. News & World Report* determined its rankings. He studied the methods used by the National Academies in awarding memberships. And he examined closely how the AAU decided to admit new members—knowledge he put to good use for the benefit of the universities he served. He was an impressive potential candidate for the UC presidency.

But when our 1995 conversation with him came to an end, Bob Grey and I were still without a clue as to its real intent.

And then we learned.

Not too long after Steve's visit, I received a curious call from UC President Jack Peltason. He telephoned, almost in apology, to tell me that the AAU had decided to admit UC Santa Barbara. But it would be only one more year before Davis would be invited to join as well, he reassured me.

About that same time, Bob Grey returned from a meeting of UC provosts, where he'd shared with Don Crawford, his Santa Barbara counterpart, that Steve Sample had been by to learn more about the campus in his bid for Peltason's job.

"That's not what he was there for," Bob recalls Crawford saying.

"It wasn't?" Bob replied.

"Noooooooo…. He was interviewing you for admission to the AAU!"

Bob recalls my reaction to this revelation: my face went white and I exhaled a choice expletive.

All in a rush, I'd understood we'd made a significant mistake—one that redounded to the entire campus.

We hadn't realized that Steve was chair of AAU's membership committee—and that a confidential preliminary study had suggested that at least two more UC campuses were ready to join UC Berkeley, UCLA and UC San Diego in the AAU. Steve had been quietly dispatched to verify UC Davis' and UC Santa Barbara's credentials for membership.

With Bob's and my frank conversation fresh on his mind, he had gone back to his membership committee and undoubtedly reported that Davis very likely was not the UC campus most ready to go into the AAU. In fact, he saw UC Santa Barbara as more deserving.

And that's what happened. UC Santa Barbara and Emory University—one public and one private as had been AAU's custom—were announced as the next members of AAU.

When we heard this at UC Davis, it hurt. We were quite certain that, if Santa Barbara had been extended an invitation, then we belonged as well.

I later learned that UCLA Chancellor Chuck Young went through the roof when the membership committee confided its new picks to the other AAU presidents. According to Chuck, most everyone with-

Bob Grey and I at an informal gathering of the Offices of the Chancellor and Provost staff in the mid-1990s.

in UC had always assumed Davis would be the next member. He didn't understand at all how UC Santa Barbara could have slipped ahead of us. I'm sorry to say that at least part of the reason had to do with my brand-new-chancellor naiveté about the AAU and what Steve Sample was up to.

Henry Yang, UC Santa Barbara's chancellor, hadn't made my mistake.

Henry and Steve Sample were friends. Perhaps they'd exchanged confidences about the reason for Steve's UCSB visit. But I know Henry wouldn't have needed a hint. There's no one better at figuring out the political circumstance and consequences for university actions. And he'd been campaigning, in a sense, for AAU membership ever since he came to UC Santa Barbara to be its chancellor.

Henry was very savvy (certainly savvier than I). In fact, he was the best of all the chancellors in scouting and recruiting prospective Nobel Prize winners, and in luring retiring Nobelists to the Santa Barbara campus for a second career. Under Henry's leadership, UCSB has had an almost miraculous increase in the number of Nobel Prize recipients—so much so, it's been running neck and neck with Berkeley.

And so it was with the AAU. Henry had determined exactly what he had to do to put Santa Barbara in the best circumstance for membership—despite not having a med school and the ready access to federal research money such schools bring. But Henry made AAU membership happen.

Just as Jack Peltason predicted, UC Davis was admitted the following year, but not without a little more drama.

By that time, Jack's successor had been chosen—Dick Atkinson, who'd been chancellor of UC San Diego. It took a decisive action on his part to open AAU's doors to both Davis and Irvine.

As UC historian Patricia Pelfrey reports in her 2012 book *The Entrepreneurial President: Richard Atkinson and the University of California, 1995-2003*:

"In 1996 the Association of American Universities demurred on adding UC Davis and UC Irvine to its ranks because the University of California already had four member campuses besides the president, who had always represented the University system at AAU meetings. Atkinson resigned to open the way for Davis and Irvine, and the AAU admitted both."

I still have the message slip from Dick's 3:50 p.m. phone call on Oct. 21, 1996: "RCA [Richard C. Atkinson] is at AAU mtg in Pasadena & wanted you to know ASAP that UCD & UCI have just been admitted to membership."

Neal Pings, AAU's president, called five minutes later to convey the happy news.

With Davis' and Irvine's election, UC's membership in AAU grew to six campuses—unprecedented among university systems. Membership in the AAU is probably the best single criterion for a research university's quality and, hands down, the University of California excels like no other.

I suppose there could still be drama ahead—though I can't really imagine so for any of UC's current AAU campuses.

But, as some former AAU members have discovered, election to this prestigious body of some 60 top research universities isn't for life.

To keep its quality bar high and its membership roster exclusively low, AAU revised its membership criteria in April 2010. For the first time, research funding for AAU institutions and nonmembers would be compared, with no guarantee that current members would continue. Essentially, for every university coming in, one would be leaving.

The University of Nebraska at Lincoln, after 102 years, was booted from the AAU in April 2011—the first time the association had ever voted a member out (two members had previously left but without such a formal nudge). Seeing Nebraska's writing on the wall, Syracuse University voluntarily withdrew shortly after.

Neither Nebraska nor Syracuse was able to persuasively meet AAU's revised criteria, which heavily favor competitively funded federal research support as well as such other measures of faculty quality as National Academy membership, major awards, publication citations, and strength in the humanities and social sciences to match science and engineering prowess.

Long-time UC Davis colleagues, Bob Grey and I teamed as the campus's chancellor and provost/executive vice chancellor from 1995 to 2001, and for 18 months before in interim roles. Bob went on to serve as acting chancellor of UC Riverside and as interim provost of the UC system. (Photo: Karin Higgins/UC Davis)

A land-grant university in a farming state, Nebraska receives much of its federal research funding by way of formulas or earmarks for agricultural studies—not through peer-reviewed grants. It's also disadvantaged when its per-faculty research award metric is calculated; the significant portion of its faculty focused on ag research is counted but their research awards are omitted. And it has no on-campus medical school to compensate by bringing in more highly valued federal funding.

University of Nebraska President Harvey Perlman fought the university's ouster but fell two votes shy. I expect he knew that he'd inevitably lose that battle, but that he had to fight in order to publicly make his points. "Our path is the right one for a socially relevant and forward-looking public research university," he said in his 2011 State of the University Address. "That path simply diverged from the new course that some AAU members had set. We'll let history judge which path will pay greater dividends."

Syracuse University similarly fell short in AAU's new accounting. Much of its research is funded by a variety of sources other than the federal government. Its then-president, Nancy Cantor, concentrated the university's efforts on revitalizing the city of Syracuse—from increasing high-school graduation rates to refurbishing city parks, converting an old warehouse into a new home for academic programs and encouraging faculty to focus their research on the city's needs.

"This is as cutting-edge research as you can get, and it's not going to show up in a narrow portfolio of federally sponsored research," Cantor told *The Chronicle of Higher Education* at the time. "The federal government can't support all the innovation we need right now."

She had a different view about what a university should be—a view that didn't fit neatly within the bounds of AAU's performance measures.

Like Syracuse, we're committed to in-the-trenches public service. Like Nebraska, we can be frustrated by the AAU's weighting of agricultural research funds. But we won't follow them out AAU's door. Of that, I'm sure.

UC Davis' measures of quality—by anyone's lights—are impressively and consistently strong and are only growing stronger by AAU's measures.

We owe our faculty for that. They got us into the AAU and they'll keep us there.

THE ASSOCIATION OF AMERICAN UNIVERSITIES

The Association of American Universities (AAU) is a nonprofit organization of 62 leading public and private research universities in the United States and Canada. Founded in 1900 to advance the international standing of U.S. research universities, AAU today focuses on issues that are important to research-intensive universities, such as funding for research, research policy issues, and graduate and undergraduate education.

MEMBER INSTITUTIONS AND YEARS OF ADMISSION

Boston University (2012)
Brandeis University (1985)
Brown University (1933)
California Institute of Technology (1934)
Carnegie Mellon University (1982)
Case Western Reserve University (1969)
Columbia University (1900)
Cornell University (1900)
Duke University (1938)
Emory University (1995)
Georgia Institute of Technology (2010)
Harvard University (1900)
Indiana University (1909)
Iowa State University (1958)
The Johns Hopkins University (1900)
Massachusetts Institute of Technology (1934)
McGill University (1926)
Michigan State University (1964)
New York University (1950)
Northwestern University (1917)
The Ohio State University (1916)
The Pennsylvania State University (1958)
Princeton University (1900)
Purdue University (1958)
Rice University (1985)
Rutgers, The State University of New Jersey (1989)
Stanford University (1900)
Stony Brook University-The State University of New York (2001)
Texas A&M University (2001)
Tulane University (1958)
The University of Arizona (1985)
University at Buffalo, The State University of New York (1989)

University of California, Berkeley (1900)
University of California, Davis (1996)
University of California, Irvine (1996)
University of California, Los Angeles (1974)
University of California, San Diego (1982)
University of California, Santa Barbara (1995)
The University of Chicago (1900)
University of Colorado Boulder (1966)
University of Florida (1985)
University of Illinois at Urbana-Champaign (1908)
The University of Iowa (1909)
The University of Kansas (1909)
University of Maryland, College Park (1969)
University of Michigan (1900)
University of Minnesota, Twin Cities (1908)
University of Missouri-Columbia (1908)
The University of North Carolina at Chapel Hill (1922)
University of Oregon (1969)
University of Pennsylvania (1900)
University of Pittsburgh (1974)
University of Rochester (1941)
University of Southern California (1969)
The University of Texas at Austin (1929)
University of Toronto (1926)
University of Virginia (1904)
University of Washington (1950)
The University of Wisconsin-Madison (1900)
Vanderbilt University (1950)
Washington University in St. Louis (1923)
Yale University (1900)

A Performing Arts Center—
On a Wing and a Prayer

Let's just do it! Let's quit talking it to death.
—BOB CELLO, VICE CHANCELLOR FOR ACADEMIC AFFAIRS, 1982-87

JUST THE RECOLLECTION MAKES ME SHUDDER—STILL. SO MANY 4 A.M. WAKE-UPS.
So much tossing and turning till the 6 a.m. alarm finally rousted me out of bed.

I announced at my 1994 inauguration that we would build a performing arts center—despite UC President Jack Peltason's sage advice to never promise anything unless you're absolutely certain you can deliver. "You're a slow learner," he told me after the speech. (Photo: UC Davis)

Deciding—and declaring at my 1994 inauguration—that the campus would finally build a center for the arts was the biggest risk I would take as chancellor. But it was a decision, and a declaration, that I knew I had to make. It was time.

The dice were pretty decisively loaded against us—strong opposition from many campus quarters, prominent regional naysayers who wanted an arts center in Sacramento (not Davis), and our fledgling fundraising track record when we had at least half of the center's $60 million price tag to raise. And, if we managed to get it built, what if it opened with the terrible acoustics that had plagued the debut of San Francisco's Davies Symphony Hall? I'd joked then that I'd be headed to the Greater Antilles, but I wasn't kidding.

So why take such a chance?

The campus had too much to lose if I didn't.

I'd first learned just how much in 1978, as a University of Illinois department head working hard to recruit a developmental biologist from Princeton. We'd pulled out all the stops—the best laboratory, the highest level of support, a remarkable salary for those days ($40,000) and our most elite faculty to help make a persuasive case. Yet my instincts and his body language in the exit interview were sending the same clear message: We had failed.

So I was stunned when this highly sought-after scientist phoned three days later to accept my offer. I'd earlier read him right, he said, but a serendipitous visit to our new Krannert Center for the Performing Arts on his way to the airport had turned his thinking around. Until he'd seen that magnificent center, he'd doubted the University of Illinois' commitment to the arts and humanities—a commitment he saw as a defining criterion of truly distinguished universities.

SPARTA OR ATHENS?

UC Berkeley learned that same recruiting lesson in the mid-1950s, when then-Chancellor Clark Kerr was brought up short by a visiting Harvard professor who felt his university's cultural life and balance between science and humanities to be far superior to Berkeley's. "I come from Athens, and I thought I'd better see what Sparta was like," he'd told Kerr.

The campus's first Center for the Arts Planning Committee, including Professor of Music D. Kern Holoman, Assistant Vice Chancellor Edwin Spafford and Department of Art Chair Richard Kramer, toured other halls in 1981. (Photo: UC Davis)

"That sort of shook me up," Kerr confided in the December 1995 issue of *California Monthly*. In response, Kerr launched construction of Zellerbach Auditorium and Playhouse and the University Art Museum, and jumpstarted funding to draw topnotch performing artists from across the nation. "So we got ourselves established as at least a minor Athens," Kerr said, "and not just a scientific Sparta."

Those few public universities that made this kind of serious commitment to the arts in the '50s, '60s and '70s consistently won the recruiting wars, snaring the elite among the best faculty—not just in the arts and humanities, but in all fields. A quality performing arts center had come to be seen as a standard fixture on the best campuses.

As UC Davis' executive vice chancellor from 1984 to 1994, I knew beyond any doubt that this increasingly noticeable gap in our constellation of quality had cost us—on occasion and across the board—our top faculty-search choices.

Predecessor chancellors Jim Meyer and Ted Hullar knew that, too, but they'd found the art-center building hurdles impossibly high. We didn't yet have the capability to raise the friends and the funds that would be necessary.

Chancellor Jim Meyer

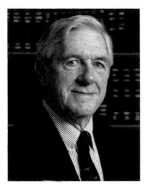

Bob Cello, vice chancellor for academic affairs

Jim kept the idea alive, though, in informal—and always animated—discussions with the deans and vice chancellors. He used to joke, "When the conversation got boring or unproductive, I'd raise the idea of a UC Davis performing arts center to stir the coals." He appointed a planning committee in 1981, received an architectural firm's report in 1984 and all the while kept a watchful eye on UC-wide facility funding.

The then-nine-campus system had just come through an eight-year building drought, and the chances of a state-funded center for the arts coming to the table had gone to zero. That meant we'd need multi-million-dollar gifts—something that didn't come easily to UC Davis with our relatively young and generally not wealthy alumni. To boot, then-UC President David Gardner thought constructing UC buildings with gift funds wasn't a good idea—it would undermine our need for the state to continue to feel an obligation to build the university's buildings.

TALKING IT TO DEATH

Still, the topic of a center for the arts continued to come up with the vice chancellors and deans, and Jim let those conversations run. One day, during one such discussion that was headed (again) toward deal-killing costs issues, Vice Chancellor for Academic Affairs and Professor of Veterinary Medicine Bob Cello exploded: "Let's just do it! Let's quit talking it to death!"

Bob pretty much shut down that particular conversation, but he got my attention. A respected academic leader and effective administrator, he was also a local performer with a great baritone voice. To this day, I have not heard a better Tevye.

His impatient advice to just "get on with it" stayed with me straight through to my inauguration speech. I'd seen the updated project planning guides and the discouraging fundraising readiness reports presented to Ted Hullar, and understood why he instead put his efforts into another worthy (and less costly, less controversial) cause—the 1993 "Students First" campaign that raised $15 million for student scholarships and fellowships. "Students First" was only our second campus-wide campaign: we'd cut our teeth on a $4 million campaign for the Buehler Alumni and Visitors Center in 1989. Could we now make an additional leap—all the way from $4 million to $15 million to $30 million?

I sure hoped so. I was counting on it, though without any reassuring preliminary data. I'd declined to undertake the fundraising feasibility study strongly advised by Rich Matheny, our vice chancellor for university relations and a seasoned fundraiser. What was the point? I was certain it would come out negative, and I didn't want that discouragement on the table as we made our plans.

So, believing the campus couldn't wait any longer, I announced at my September 28, 1994, inauguration that we would build a performing arts center that "will symbolically and practically stand as UC Davis' commitment to the arts and humanities…. It is a facility that we must have."

It was a declaration that countered longtime friend and UC President Jack Peltason's sage advice to me to never promise anything unless you're absolutely certain you can deliver. I did it anyway, believing—hoping—that sheer determination would trump adversity. "You're a slow learner," Jack told me after the speech.

AN "EDIFICE COMPLEX"

The campus's reaction didn't boost my confidence. There were supporters, without doubt, but their numbers were, well, small.

Too many others saw reasons for not building such a center—too expensive ("We're going to build that when we could be building this?"), a fruitless display of UC Berkeley envy ("When will we get it? Berkeley is Berkeley and we are not; we shouldn't be ashamed of being Davis."), an unwise wandering from our agricultural roots ("The more we put into the arts and humanities, the less we'll have for our bread and butter—plant and animal science."), and a reckless disregard for mounting deferred-maintenance problems.

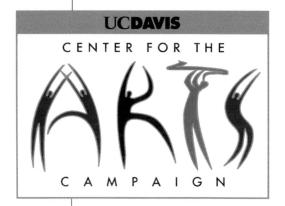

And those were my friends!

Others talked about my "edifice complex."

And still others—no fewer than five UC Davis Foundation Board members, our staunchest and most generous allies—wrote with politely expressed concerns about the wisdom of this project. They, more than anyone, knew how high we'd need to set our fundraising bar in a region with a dearth of corporate headquarters, with philanthropic giving below the national average, and with efforts already underway for a Sacramento arts complex. And they knew our limited donor base and the likely resistance of deans to having their supporters "poached" for this campus-wide project.

Asking for their trust and their help, I pushed on, appointing a planning committee in 1995.

The committee recommended a major performance venue of 1,500-1,800 seats, a smaller recital hall/technology classroom, and a visual arts center—and that the projects be phased.

Customized shovels, with cello necks for handles, helped us break ground in May 2000. Pictured from left, Campus Planning Assistant Vice Chancellor Bob Segar; Humanities, Arts and Cultural Studies Dean Elizabeth Langland; University Relations Associate Vice Chancellor Gina Kelsch; Professor of Music/University Choruses Director Jeffrey Thomas; Professor of Music/UC Davis Symphony Conductor D. Kern Holoman; UC Davis Cultural Programs Director Brian McCurdy; Sacramento Ballet President-Elect John Webre; Rosalie Vanderhoef; and Professor of Dramatic Art Sue Ellen Case. (Photo: Neil Michel/Axiom)

We'd start with the performance hall (to be funded evenly by philanthropic gifts and by non-state campus monies) and the recital hall/technology classroom (we'd seek state construction funds). The visual arts center would follow when funds permitted—a welcome delay, I knew, for key Sacramento benefactors who were leading a campaign to expand the Crocker Art Museum and feared we'd be dipping into the pockets of their potential donors. With this concession, they'd stand down in their opposition to our performing arts center plan.

I'd tucked away some non-state funds in anticipation of our project, intending we'd have about half the performance hall's expected $60 million cost covered when we launched our campaign.

Even so, I wasn't sleeping well. I worried about our ability to raise the other half.

SLOW-GOING FUNDRAISING

I knew we had loyal and enthusiastic volunteers who'd help us succeed (volunteers like Hal and Carol Sconyers, who stepped up to chair the stakeholders phase of the campaign and who I knew would see this project all the way through). And I knew that my wife, Rosalie, a former schoolteacher, would make a passionate and persuasive case to donors about how regional schoolchildren would be absolutely transfixed by the center's performances—and exposed not just to the arts but to college.

Nonetheless, we had a daunting task and, not sur-

Rosalie Vanderhoef collects tickets from schoolchildren attending an October 1997 UC Davis Presents matinee performance in the Main Theatre. (Photo: Sue Cockrell/The Davis Enterprise)

Two construction workers shake hands at the March 2001 "topping out" ceremony celebrating the placement of the center's last steel beam. (Photo: UC Davis)

prisingly, our fundraising was slow-going.

We had not quite $9 million in the bank by the time we'd publicly launched our $30 million campaign in January 1999—an OK start but we really needed to pick up the pace.

We broke ground in May 2000, with only $12 million raised, far shy of our mid-campaign goal. But Rumsey Indian Rancheria (now Yocha Dehe Wintun Nation) Tribal Council Chair Paula Lorenzo that day announced a $600,000 gift to name the arts center's grand lobby—at that point, our largest private donation and a reason to celebrate. The gift was a much-needed boost, and we hoped the council's generosity would inspire others.

Construction was now beginning, with no hot prospects for a $10 million building-naming donor and less than half the needed funds raised—a fact that didn't go unnoticed by *The Davis Enterprise* in a Nov. 13, 2000, front-page story titled "Campus' arts fund-raising is lagging."

I wasn't the only one disturbed by that headline—so was Barbara Jackson, long-time arts supporter and volunteer who designed and sewed costumes for the Sacramento Opera and local theatre groups. She'd signed on early to give and solicit gifts for the arts center, and was concerned we weren't making greater progress.

So, at our March 27, 2001, "topping out" ceremony to celebrate the placement of the center's last steel beam, Barbara announced a $5 million commitment—an eye-popping contribution that breathed new life into our fundraising effort and helped us believe the center really would happen. In appreciation, we named the center's 1,800-seat main hall for Barbara and her late husband, renowned American West history professor W. Turrentine "Turpie" Jackson, who sadly had died just a few days after groundbreaking. She signed both their names on the last beam just before it was hoisted into place.

I remember talking with Barbara about the unexpected new wealth that made her major gift possible. For many years, Turpie had worked as a consulting historian for Wells Fargo Bank and such agencies as the National Park Service and the California Department of Parks and Recreation. He'd set aside that extra money in a retirement account that had done very well—just how well came as a surprise to Barbara. Of her new-found money, she told me very simply, "The university needs it, and I don't."

She and Turpie had given steadily and generously of their time and money since their 1951 arrival on campus, with the arts a special love for Barbara. She would often quote St. Augustine to explain their gifts: "Where your pleasure is, there is your treasure; where your treasure, there your heart; where your heart, there your happiness."

Barbara Jackson announced an eye-popping $5 million commitment at our March 2001 "topping out" ceremony, breathing new life into our fundraising effort. (Photo: UC Davis)

Barbara had certainly made us happy with her $5 million gift. It marked a turning point in our campaign, lifting us to $17.3 million in gifts. We were immensely grateful.

As construction continued, we inched up to $20 million but then seemed to hit a wall. We still needed that elusive $10 million donor in whose honor the building would be named.

I again was not sleeping well.

But three months after our topping-out ceremony, we learned quite unexpectedly of a promising new possibility.

A $10 MILLION NAME

In May 2001, a trio of us—Neal Van Alfen (dean of the College of Agricultural and Environmental Sciences), Jim Wolpert (chair of the Department of Viticulture and Enology), and I—met in Napa with Robert Mondavi's business advisers Frank Farella and Terry Eager about a hoped-for gift to bring our wine and food programs together in a new building and to construct a new winery. We emphasized the importance of combining the study of food and wine (there'd be better education, research and outreach), and mentioned the possible proximity of these new facilities to the under-construction performing arts center. What we were creating, we told Frank and Terry, was essentially the academic reflection of what the Mondavis were building in Napa—Copia: The American Center for Wine, Food and the Arts. That "happy confluence," as Frank expressed it, resonated.

Anticipating perhaps $5 million to $10 million, we were quite amazed to hear that Bob was ready to commit as much as $25 million to our wine and food programs. He was grateful for UC Davis' partnership in building the international reputation of the California wine industry, and for the many UC Davis graduates who had worked in his winery. And he was ready to express that gratitude in a very major way. We were thrilled. And I was hopeful that maybe an arts-center seed had been planted. Likely a long shot, I thought, given Bob's already extraordinary generosity, but I had to hope.

The next month, that seed had begun to sprout. I learned there could possibly be another Mondavi gift. My good friend and frequent lunch partner, former UC Regent Roy Brophy, and Mondavi accountant Terry Eager both held seats on the UC Davis Graduate School of Management Board. Terry knew there was a possibility that the Mondavis would additionally contribute $10 million to name the Center for the Arts, but he didn't know whom to contact about it. Roy knew.

The center's soaring steel frame rises from the ground in March 2001, anchoring the campus's new south entry and sitting kitty-corner to the Buehler Alumni and Visitors Center. (Photo: D. Kern Holoman/UC Davis)

I was VERY happy and hopeful at Roy's news, but still not daring to count any chickens. I didn't even tell Rosalie that we anticipated signing a $10 million Memorandum of Understanding with Bob and Margrit when they visited campus on Aug. 17, 2001. She just knew we would be driving them by the intended site for the Robert Mondavi Institute for Wine and Food Science and viewing the under-construction arts center from the top deck of the parking structure, then chatting over lunch.

I have a very clear memory of Margrit's quick absorption of the whole scene as she looked out her car window at the Center for the Arts coming out of the ground. Its eventual size was already apparent and she was impressed.

There's no doubt Margrit was the major force behind the performing arts portion of the eventual Mondavi naming gift. She appreciated the arts and was a long-time participant. Not long after she joined the winery in 1967, she initiated the first of what came to be wine industry benchmark programs in the arts, including art shows, music festivals and classical concerts. She and Bob believed passionately in enhancing life through wine, food and the arts. And now they had an opportunity to integrate and support all three—to transform the experience they had created in Napa into a legacy of education for generations to come—by naming both the Institute for Wine and Food Science and the nearby Center for the Arts.

And from the deck of the parking structure, a stone's throw from I-80 and its tens of

Margrit and Robert Mondavi finalize a $35 million gift agreement on Sept. 19, 2001, flanked by Mondavi attorney Frank Farella, UC Davis Director of Planned Giving Rick Vorpe and me. (Photo: Neil Michel/Axiom)

thousands of daily passing cars, I knew that Bob was also making a smart business calculation. He could imagine the freeway signs, the ads, the programs, the many co-branding opportunities. As Margrit told me years later, "Bob was always so proud of [the Mondavi Center] and felt it was the best money we ever spent."

So our Mrak Hall lunch that day turned out to be another happy occasion. Neal remembers it as "just pure joy." And Assistant Vice Chancellor for Campus Planning Bob Segar, our indefatigable point person for the center, emailed me after the meeting, "I hurt myself trying to do a cartwheel."

At lunch, I'd told Bob and Margrit that it would mean so much to have the Mondavi name on both the institute and the arts center. Referring to his business as a "test tube" winery, Bob in many ways acted like a university, I'd said. Contrary to the normal business mode, his winemaking research was an open book, available to every vintner—very similar to the university's research. And, like UC Davis, he prized innovation and excellence without compromise. To have the Mondavi name associated with UC Davis would be the perfect pairing of two great names, I told him. And then I paused, waiting for his response.

It came quickly and simply: "Let's do it!"

The pronouncement called for a toast—unfortunately something we hadn't prepared for. Luckily Neal's office was just downstairs, where he had a stash of cabernet from our

Oakville Experimental Vineyard. But he didn't have wineglasses. And plastic cups wouldn't do. Clear glass coffee mugs passed muster, and we lifted them in celebration of our agreement.

Rosalie, who'd been working so hard to make the center a reality and hadn't expected an MOU to be signed that day, recalls that she was "kind of shocked and thinking, 'My gosh, this is really happening.'" She remembers, too, that after we'd profusely thanked Bob and Margrit they in turn were thanking us for the opportunity. "I just felt it was all so right."

Margrit gave us each a special memento of the occasion—signed coaster doodles of Bacchus, the god of the grape harvest, winemaking and wine. Neal noticed her coaster doodle first and asked her to sign it. She was happy to oblige, and sketched and signed coasters for us all.

PROJECT M

With the MOU signed Aug. 17, 2001, we quietly began our preparations for a Sept. 19 public announcement of the Mondavis' $35 million gift—$25 million for the Robert Mondavi Institute for Wine and Food Science and $10 million for the Robert and Margrit Mondavi Center for the Performing Arts. It was the largest gift the campus had ever received, and one of the most generous in UC's history.

There were still i's to dot and t's to cross with the UC Regents and the Office of the President, and we didn't want to let word slip before the Mondavis were ready. But we had planning to do—pronto—so we instantly got to work, coding our emails and meeting agendas "Project M" and bringing people in on a strictly "need to know" basis.

On Sept. 11, just a week before our intended announcement, terrorists struck this country. We questioned whether we should go forward with our event—which was to include Gov. Gray Davis, whose security detail would be on heightened alert. Ultimately, we decided we should, just as the University of California hadn't shut down on 9-11. We didn't want to add yet one more thing to the terrorists' list of accomplishments. We would wear special ribbons signaling our sorrow for the victims and their families and our belief in the country's resilience.

Just two days before our announcement, the governor's advance team nixed our intended news conference site—the upper deck of the parking structure, chosen because it afforded a view of both the institute and the arts center sites. It presented too many security challenges, we were told. So we scrambled again, settling on the courtyard of the Buehler Alumni and Visitors Center (AVC).

The day before the event, we'd alerted news media but, at the Mondavis' request, didn't reveal their names or the gift amount. That was to wait till the news conference. But, unfortunately, the governor's press office leaked the information later that afternoon.

We were mortified and held our breath for any repercussions.

The next morning (Sept. 19, 2001), just before the news conference, Neal walked the Mondavis into a meeting of his college's faculty in the AVC's AGR Hall and announced their jaw-dropping, multi-million-dollar gift. Faculty immediately leapt to their feet, and the packed room erupted in thunderous applause—applause so prolonged that Bob and Margrit had a hard time quieting everyone so they could speak. It was a euphoric moment (with the exception of one faculty member's expressed disapproval when he learned where the institute would be sited, but he was clearly a lone, and distanced, voice. His colleagues were ecstatic.).

On we went to the 10:30 a.m. news conference in the AVC Courtyard where absolutely thrilled campus folks gathered with news media and regional dignitaries. I particularly remember UC President Dick Atkinson's spot-on analogy that "Robert Mondavi is to the California wine industry what the three tenors are to opera, Cal Ripken (Jr.) is to baseball and the University of California is to California education." And I remember, with some chagrin and amusement, Gov. Gray Davis' whispered stage instruction to me to swap chairs with him while he was up at the podium. I didn't understand at first, but

Gov. Gray Davis let me know he would take my chair when he returned from the podium because it was in better view of the news cameras. (Photo: Neil Michel/Axiom)

he didn't hesitate to tell me why—my chair was in better view of the news cameras.

But no one was more photographed or celebrated that day than the Mondavis. And they generously shared that spotlight with the campus, letting the world know through their gift that UC Davis was a university worthy of investment and with great strengths across the spectrum. They had confidence in us to do wonderful things…with their wonderful gift.

SNEAK PEEKS

Working six—then seven—days a week in the homestretch of preparing the Mondavi Center for its Oct. 3, 2002, grand opening, construction workers seemed to me to have "caught the fever." In a way, the center had become their facility just like it

Our Oct. 2, 2002, "Celebrating the Arts" Fall Convocation was our campus family's first chance to experience the new hall—and they filled it to the brim. (Photo: UC Davis)

was ours. We treated them and their families to a T-shirt-and-jeans "Hard Hat Concert" by the UC Davis Symphony Orchestra on Sept. 28. It was a way to say "thank you" and to give the hall a test run.

And what a thrill that performance must have been for our symphony orchestra—especially for conductor and music professor D. Kern Holoman. Kern had served on virtually every art center planning committee, all the way back to 1981. And now here he was at the finish line, baton in one hand and a construction hat in the other. He strode out on Jackson Hall's stage, shook the hard hat high in the air, and the appreciative audience just erupted. "It was a big, big moment," recalls Jeremy Ganter, now the Mondavi Center's associate executive director. "We were transitioning out of construction to the real deal."

I surprised campus planner Bob Segar at Fall Convocation by conspiring to have his 16-year-old daughter, Andrea, an accomplished violinist, be the Mondavi Center's first solo performer. (Photo: Allison Portello/The Davis Enterprise)

Our faculty, staff, students and special campus friends had their preview chance at our Oct. 2 "Celebrating the Arts" Fall Convocation. The moment the doors opened, they streamed in, filling all three levels of the 1,800-seat hall, eager to experience this wonderful new facility.

I carry two special memories of that day.

The first: a blessing ceremony by Native American Studies Professor George Longfish honoring the spirits of the 14 Patwin Indians whose remains were disturbed during the site's excavation. This land was their ancestral home ("then, now and always"), and we knew we'd been given a great privilege to perpetuate the traditions of music and dance that were first celebrated on this ground more than 500 years ago. Fanning smoke with a feather, Professor Longfish performed the blessing and expressed hope that the Mondavi Center would become a place where understanding and wisdom would flourish. (Patwin Elder Bill Wright also blessed the center at the next day's ribbon-cutting, followed by a performance of traditional California Indian dance.)

And the second special memory: an emotional surprise for campus planner Bob Segar, who, night and day, had lived the Mondavi Center from its beginning (he ended all his emails with the exhortation "Get the Hall!"). I'd conspired with Bob's wife, Jenifer, and their 16-year-old daughter, Andrea (an accomplished violinist), for Andrea to be the center's first solo performer. I'd sneaked her into Convocation through a back door and stunned Bob when I called her out on stage. Before a packed house, with an assurance and a calm that belied her years, she performed Paganini's Caprice No. 20 on her circa-1623 violin. Bob was moved to tears. "I was lucky I was breathing," he says today. "When I walk in that building, I'm luckier than anybody. I get to re-live that moment every time."

A DAZZLING CHRISTENING

Christening day—Thursday, Oct. 3— dawned clear and bright, with relief from the north wind that had whipped through campus the two days prior. It was a perfect fall day—the perfect setting for gala opening festivities that would last the weekend long and mark a major milestone in the campus's and the region's history.

Among the day's most memorable moments for me:

• A mid-morning, giant-scissors ribbon-cutting capped by an ooh-and-aah performance of Project Bandaloop—six acrobatic dancers (tethered to ropes and accompanied by a ledge-perched fiddler) who spun, twisted and cartwheeled on the south face of the Mondavi Center.

• Bob Mondavi's utter delight as he stepped on stage and for the first time gazed out at

Project Bandaloop's acrobatic dancers spun, twisted and cartwheeled on the Mondavi Center's south face during the center's opening weekend. (Photo: UC Davis)

The Mondavi Center sparkles as opening-night attendees arrive for the inaugural concert by the San Francisco Symphony, which also opened Freeborn Hall 40 years earlier. (Photo: Debbie Aldridge/UC Davis)

a completed Jackson Hall: "This is huge. This is amazing. This is way beyond any expectation."

• The grandness of the building, dramatically outlined in sparkling lights against the night sky.

• Black ties and top hats and floor-length gowns in abundance at that evening's inaugural concert by the San Francisco Symphony (a reprised role for the orchestra, which had also played at Freeborn Hall's dedication 40 years earlier).

• Campus labor union picketing as news media and gala guests arrived. (But I was grateful our unionized employees ultimately decided on an informational picket rather than a strike, which would have deep-sixed the San Francisco Symphony's performance.)

• The excited, pre-performance buzz as concert-goers gathered in the center's dramatic lobby, made their way up the grand staircase, and, for the first time, stepped inside Jackson Hall and took it all in—the Douglas fir paneling and India sandstone that warmly wrapped the entire room, the expansiveness of the stage, the impressive, three-tiered house of 1,800 seats that still managed to feel intimate. That first glimpse was truly breathtaking.

• And, to my great relief, the hall's beautiful richness and clarity of sound. I wouldn't need to flee to the Greater Antilles after all!

It was as near-perfect as an evening could be. If only Jim Meyer and Bob Cello could have been with us—that would have been perfection.

Jim had had the opportunity to turn a shovel at groundbreaking, but sadly he'd died just nine days after the Mondavi Center's gala opening. And we'd lost Bob a year earlier.

I'm reminded that on that near-perfect night I'd told a local reporter that "I feel like somebody's looking down on us and saying, 'You deserve this.'"

Hmmmm…. Maybe, just maybe, it was a perfect night after all.

▶ http://escholarship.org/uc/ucdavischancelloremeritus_books

Mondavi Center Opening Buzz

"You have a wonderful new instrument—this hall—and we enjoyed the experience of playing it for the first time."—**Michael Tilson Thomas**, San Francisco Symphony conductor

"It's absolutely overwhelming. It's so beautiful and the sound…!"—Philanthropist **Barbara Jackson**, for whom Jackson Hall is named

"Great musicians want to come to halls like this. It sounds as good as it looks. I feel like I've been transported. I could be in Sydney; I could be in New York; I could be in Davis."—Sacramento County Supervisor **Muriel Johnson**

"The University of California at Davis has really done it, capping its 50 year transformation from a small ag campus to a major university with the inauguration of the Mondavi Center for the Performing Arts on Thursday."—**Robert Commanday**, *San Francisco Classical Voice*, Oct. 8, 2002

"It exceeds any expectations we might have had. Although people are excited right now, they may have very little concept of what this building will mean over the years to this region…. People travel long distances to a facility like this…and you have it in your own backyard! And remember that the possibility for young people to experience the arts in a facility like this is so important."—**Jim Wockenfuss**, retired director of UC Davis' University Cultural Programs

Some 15,000 school children visit the Mondavi Center each year, attending matinee performances, touring the building, and participating in master classes and workshops. (Photo: UC Davis)

"If there is such a thing as a cultural convert, than I am most certainly it. The Mondavi Center proved itself in my eyes—normal college eyes—to be amazing and worthwhile…. I discovered the meaning of classical music and…classical art…. Go and make it your own. It is there for the taking."—**Aaron A. Davidson**, *The California Aggie* arts editor, Oct. 4, 2002

"Unbelievable. This is unbelievable. It tells me Davis is no longer just an ag school. This campus is on the move and is going to change this region forever. Life will never be the same in the Sacramento region after tonight."—**Steve Weiss**, former director of UC Davis' University Cultural Programs

"I was amazed at the beauty of it and how large it was and yet it felt comfortable. Soon I began to fall in love with it."—**Robert Mondavi**

"The proof is in the pudding. What an occasion to celebrate. We're going to be here as often as we can."—**Margrit Mondavi**

"Several people have told me it exceeded their wildest expectations. It's truly an amazing structure…. I think it will become one of the symbols of Northern California."—**Brian McCurdy**, Mondavi Center's first director

"I've got a mailbox full of cards and letters saying this is a golden moment for us. I believe it's true."—**D. Kern Holoman**, professor of music and UC Davis Symphony conductor

"The acoustics exceed even my expectations. The hall has not only the carrying power for big sounds, but yesterday there was a duet for viola and cello and it was the most beautiful sound, with even just those two instruments."—**Ross Bauer**, music department chair

"It's in very good taste. Clean lines. I love it."—**Richard Brunelle**, Davis High School 30-year music director

"I followed the construction of this building with great interest. I must say the final project is quite stunning. No one will ever whiz by on I-80 without making a firm mental note of the presence of the University of California, Davis."—UC President **Richard Atkinson**

"When I come back to campus, it will still be here, and I can say I was here when it opened."—Fourth-year student **Sean Soares**

"I love to think that this glorious lighted building, visible to travelers on Interstate 80 as they pass our campus, is inviting them to stop and visit."—**Elizabeth Langland**, dean of the Division of Humanities, Arts and Cultural Studies

"It was an absolutely perfect evening—the concert hall is wonderful, the building is grand, the whole experience everything one could ask for. And I thought, too, that the audience…was transformed by the place, the ambiance, the sense that we were indeed at a major university for a major cultural event…. The Mondavi Center is the best thing that has happened to the Davis campus since I've been here."—**Max Byrd**, professor emeritus of English

"It's beautiful, wonderful—the sound is exquisite, the acoustics are perfect, the hall is sparkling and gorgeous."—**Susan Mann**, professor emerita of history

"…the stature of this region has permanently risen…. Larry and Rosalie Vanderhoef, modest Midwesterners by birth, kept faith with a dream."—*Sacramento Business Journal* "Mt. Mondavi" editorial, Oct. 4, 2002

"After 43 years of designing buildings, I retired at the end of 2013. I get asked all the time what my favorite building is, and I never hesitate: The Mondavi Center."—Architect **Stan Boles** (in 2014)

The 2012 Fall Convocation—celebrating the Mondavi Center's 10th anniversary— provided an opportunity for me to greet Chancellor Linda Katehi and Margrit Mondavi at the reception that followed. (Photo: Sue Cockrell/The Davis Enterprise)

Mondavi Center Quick Facts

• 104,000-square-foot performing arts facility with state-of-the-art lighting and sound systems
• Opened October 2002
• Easily accessible and visible just off Interstate 80
• $60.9 million cost ($57 million for construction, $3.9 million for initial endowment and for program and start-up costs) financed through combination of campus funds and $31 million in private gifts
• 1,801-seat Barbara K. and W. Turrentine Jackson Hall
• 250-seat Larry and Rosalie Vanderhoef Studio Theatre
• BOORA Architects from Portland, Oregon (whose chief architect Stan Boles gave shape and form to our vision of a center for the performing arts)
• McKay, Conant and Brook (whose master acoustician Ron McKay gave our vision a voice)
• McCarthy Building Companies, Inc. (whose workers made our vision a reality)
• Interior paneling: century-old Douglas fir salvaged from the bottom of freshwater Ruby Lake in British Columbia
• Exterior wall material: sandstone from India
• Double-wall construction, with two feet of air space separating the inner and outer walls
• A basement under Jackson Hall and a "technical attic" at the ceiling, creating a "box within a box" for acoustical isolation from train and freeway vibrations
• Highest point (the stage's flytower): 100 feet
• Three-story, 75-foot high lobby

A waterproofing problem was corrected in 2011-12. A faulty membrane was replaced, and some 50,000 new sandstone tiles brought in from the original quarry in India. UC bore no cost. (Photo: Gregory Urquiaga/ UC Davis)

All Three Dreams Coming True

It took a while, but all three dreams of the original Center for the Arts vision (announced at my 1994 inauguration) are coming true.

And we have Margrit Mondavi and Barbara Jackson to thank, once again.

With the performance hall accomplished, they set out to interest like-minded arts benefactors in our long-awaited art museum and recital hall/classroom building.

With their help, ground was broken in 2014 for both these facilities.

Margrit introduced her friends Jan Shrem and Maria Manetti Shrem to our art museum project and made an early $2 million gift herself. Jan, the founder of the Clos Pegase winery in Napa Valley, followed her lead, contributing $10 million in 2011. The Jan Shrem and Maria Manetti Shrem Museum of Art will be located kitty-corner to the Mondavi Center, completing the campus' south entry. We'll have yet another architecturally stunning building to catch the eye of I-80 travelers! (Remember when the water tower was our most prominent landmark?)

Barbara introduced her longtime friends and music lovers Grace and Grant Noda to the recital hall/classroom project and also made a bequest herself. The Nodas

The Jan Shrem and Maria Manetti Shrem Museum of Art will complete the campus' south entry, visible to I-80 travelers. (Rendering: SO - IL and Bohlin Cywinski Jackson, Associated Architects)

contributed $1.5 million toward the 399-seat recital hall's construction. The lobby will be named in the Noda family's honor, and the stage will be named for Barbara.

This beautiful new building will sit at the east entrance to campus, where the old boiler plant and Temporary Building 195 once stood. It's the last Center for the Arts piece to fall into place.

I'm so grateful for the remarkable generosity of Margrit and Barbara, of the Shrems and the Nodas (and, most recently, of the late Ann Pitzer, who donated $5 million for the recital hall/classroom building).

They'd be the first to tell you, though, that the job's not yet done—not while there are collections to build, programs to support, and endowments to fund.

But, together, we'll achieve that, too. Because we've never just built for today, for ourselves; we've always had our eye on tomorrow, on sustaining what we've built for generations to come.

The Classroom and Recital Hall, to be named the Ann E. Pitzer Center, will sit at the east entrance to campus where the old boiler plant and Temporary Building 195 once stood. (Rendering: LPAS Architects)

The Saddest Time

This was a heartbreaking tragedy.… The people that died out there loved where they were and they loved what they were doing, and they gave their lives for it.
—PATTY WEST, RESEARCH EXPEDITION AND RESCUE TEAM MEMBER
AT MARCH 30, 2000, SACRAMENTO AIRPORT NEWS CONFERENCE

I CAN'T REMEMBER A TIME OF MORE PROFOUND SADNESS.

Our shock quickly turned to grief as word slowly—agonizingly so—reached the campus from a tiny, one-public-telephone village in remote Baja California.

A sudden storm's wind-whipped waves had capsized one of our research boats in Mexico's Sea of Cortez, and the fate of the nine aboard, including three visiting scientists from Kyoto University, was unclear.

Five Japanese and American researchers lost their lives in the Sea of Cortez tragedy. (Photo collage: UC Davis)

News Service Director Lisa Lapin brought us first word, interrupting our standing Tuesday (March 28, 2000) morning meeting of the Council of Vice Chancellors in 203 Mrak Hall.

There'd been a boat accident, she reported. Bodies had been recovered. Survivors had been found. People were still missing (including expedition leader Gary Polis, chair of our environmental science and policy department). And the U.S. Coast Guard didn't yet have permission to join the search-and-rescue effort.

Her sparse information came from Polis' just-alerted department.

Though stunned and with little detail, we recognized we needed to do two things immediately: Ask U.S. Sen. Dianne Feinstein and Congressman Doug Ose to help the U.S. Coast Guard gain the Mexican government's permission to join the search. And get ourselves down to Baja to bring the survivors back.

With Feinstein and Ose pulling great and mighty strings, the Coast Guard was working alongside the Mexican Navy later that day. And Neal Van Alfen, dean of the College of Agricultural and Environmental Sciences, that morning dispatched Bob Brewer (an information systems manager in Polis' department with search-and-rescue and law-enforcement experience) to Baja to provide leadership, obtain reliable information and bring the survivors home.

Little more than an hour after word first reached us, the U.S. Coast Guard issued a press release verifying the accident and triggering a flood of media calls to our News Service at a rate of about 200 an hour, soon followed by calls from concerned family, friends and colleagues from across the globe. Almost immediately, officials from the Japanese Consulate in San Francisco arrived at Mrak Hall, urgently seeking information about the fate of the three Kyoto University researchers. Neal invited them to sit with him in his office for the better part of two days "so that they knew what we knew and to build trust."

News Service Director Lisa Lapin briefed reporters multiple times as the tragedy unfolded. (Photo: Wayne Tilcock/The Davis Enterprise)

We issued our first media advisory at noon that day—to be followed by more than 17 different news releases and several on-the-steps-of-Mrak news briefings as the tragedy unfolded. Our News Service staff worked double shifts to respond to U.S. media during the day and Japanese media overnight as news trickled in from U.S. embassy officials, the Coast Guard and survivor accounts. A special Web page logged more than 13,000 separate visits in just three days.

Here's what we learned and shared early that week:

Gary Polis—an internationally renowned scorpion expert and ecologist—had taken a group of UC Davis students, Japanese visiting scholars and Earthwatch Institute study-tour participants to Mexico to study the ecology of spiders and scorpions that inhabit the islands of the Sea of Cortez. Expedition members left the town of Pueblo de Bahia de Los Angeles, about 300 miles south of San Diego, Calif., on Monday morning (March 27, 2000) in two boats to conduct research on several islands about five nautical miles off shore. A few hours later, as the wind and waves picked up, both boats headed back to port. Midway, Polis' motorboat flooded and capsized, pitching its nine passengers into the choppy sea. When the crew of the second boat arrived at port and realized Polis' boat hadn't returned, they set out in search, thinking he'd sought shelter in a cove. Unsuccessful, they reported the missing boat to Mexican officials at 10:30 Monday night.

On Tuesday morning, four survivors had been found on two nearby islands: UC Davis post-graduate researcher Gary Huxel, 38; undergraduate Sarah Ratay, 20; and graduate students Becca Lewison, 28, and Ralph Haygood, 35. Two bodies had been recovered: that of UC Davis post-graduate researcher Michael Rose, 27, and an unidentified Japanese researcher. And three remained missing.

By Wednesday, two of the three Japanese scientists (considered to be among their country's leading ecologists) had been found and declared dead—Takuya Abe, 55, and Masahiko Higashi, 45. The third—Shigeru Nakano, 37—and Gary Polis, 53, remained missing and were presumed dead.

A Mexican Army boat heads for Isla Cabeza de Caballo to search for survivors of the capsized research boat. (Photo: Denis Poroy/Associated Press)

(Gary was thought by the survivors to have suffered a heart attack in the water.)

On Thursday, we learned Gary's body had been found. But Shigeru Nakano remained missing—and remains so today, despite an extended search by the Mexican Navy and Army, the U.S. Coast Guard, and local Mexican fishing and diving boats, as well as additional efforts by his family.

BRINGING THE SURVIVORS HOME

Much of our updated news came from Bob Brewer, who, at Neal's request, flew to San Diego that Tuesday, shortly after we'd learned of the accident. He took with him Francisco "Paco" Sanchez-Pinero, a native Spanish speaker who'd worked with Polis and knew the area, and student assistant Nate Roth, who also had search-and-rescue training. In a borrowed UC San Diego van, they sped along 300 miles of dark and rutted roads south of the San Diego border to the village of San Quintin. Along the way, "we got stopped by the Federales because I passed them," Brewer said. Sanchez-Pinero smoothed things over and they were quickly en route again, arriving about 12:30 a.m.

All the while, Brewer stayed in touch with Neal, reporting what he learned and following Neal's instruction to "do whatever you can and get everyone home safely."

"Neal was my hero," Brewer recalls. "He'd told me, 'Call me along the way. Whatever you need, I'll make it happen. None of 'be careful what you say, there may be liability issues.' He was completely human. His concern was taking care of these people."

Family and friends greeted accident survivors as they arrived by chartered plane at Sacramento International Airport. (Photo: Florence Low/The Davis Enterprise)

Neal says it was Brewer's performance that was "really amazing," a compliment Brewer shrugs off with "I happened to have a skill set that was handy at the time."

Early that next morning (Wednesday), the news media (including a Japanese film crew and a helicoptered-in Associated Press reporter) started arriving at the village, hoping to interview the four survivors. "They were traumatized," Brewer says of the four. "We did our best to keep them isolated if they didn't want to be interviewed." Instead, he fielded reporters' questions and, with his team, joined the rescue efforts, scouring the area in a small aircraft and buying gasoline for some of the local searchers.

The next morning (Thursday), a caravan of seven vehicles set out for the San Diego border, the first leg in bringing our surviving expedition members home.

We'd chartered a plane to fly them from San Diego's Lindbergh Field Airport to Sacramento International Airport. But we would first meet them at the border—at Otay Mesa, a more lightly traveled crossing where they would be interviewed by the U.S. Coast Guard before we could shepherd them away. (Our group included Neal, assistant deans Tom Kaiser and Connie Melendy, environmental science and policy professor Paul Sabatier, public communications director Maril Stratton and me). I'd hoped that our being there, awaiting their arrival, might offer them some measure of comfort. They were part of our UC Davis family, and we were all hurting.

They arrived at the border in the early afternoon, looking drained and emotionally spent. We had a few moments together before they needed to meet with U.S. Coast Guard investigators to discuss the accident and before I needed to return to the airport to meet the arriving families of the Japanese researchers and representatives of Los Angeles' Japanese consulate.

We would reconnect several hours later at the airport as we prepared to board a chartered plane for Sacramento. But before our flight, two of the survivors (Becca Lewison and Gary Huxel) and one member of the rescue team (Patty West) joined me, Neal and Counseling Center director Judy Mack during our meeting with the Japanese researchers' grieving families, who were desperate for first-hand information about the tragedy. It was an excruciating gathering, a wrenching hour of agonizing conversation, of pleas for reassurance that a missing husband and father was still alive.

When we ultimately parted, the families continued their sorrowful travels to Mexico to retrieve the bodies of Professors Abe and Higashi, with Professor Nakano's wife and parents still harboring hope that he would be found.

Our UC Davis group proceeded to the Lindbergh Field tarmac to board a chartered DeHaviland turboprop airplane, whose pilot and crew were patiently awaiting our arrival. They'd had to file several amended flight plans as our expected departure had been delayed by longer-than-anticipated border debriefings and by extended discussions with the Japanese families.

Once we were in the air early that evening, Judy visited with each of the survivors, acknowledging the difficult emotional path ahead and encouraging them to take advantage of the Counseling Center's services when they returned to campus. And Maril probed their willingness (and ultimately helped Gary and Becca prepare) to speak briefly at an anticipated airport news conference intended to serve as the survivors' sole public comment on the tragedy.

AIRPORT NEWS CONFERENCE

A few minutes before 9 p.m., our Le Bas International plane touched down at Sacramento International Airport. Illumined by television camera lights, buses carrying the survivors' family and friends were waiting on the windy tarmac to transport us all to a secluded area in Terminal A. With tears, hugs, and one brief laugh, it was an overwhelmingly quiet and somber return and reunion.

Survivors Gary Huxel and Becca Lewison (center) and rescue organizer Patty West addressed reporters at a late-night airport press conference. (Photo: Florence Low/The Davis Enterprise)

Gary, Becca, rescue organizer Patty West, Neal, Maril and I proceeded to a crowded interior room in the airport for a late-hour news conference. Periodically pausing to maintain his composure, Gary told reporters, "We want everybody to know that Michael and Gary gave their lives in helping to save people who were involved in this accident. Both of them wore themselves out, physically, emotionally and mentally. Gary's heart just gave out. And Michael was just so devastated, felt so responsible for the loss that it killed him, literally killed him. He struggled so hard to get help, to keep the Japanese scientists with the boat and keep them alive."

Becca, looking dazed and staring straight ahead, briefly described the boat's capsizing by "a wall of water. Despite flotation devices, it was difficult to stay afloat, and over time we became separated into smaller groups. After three or four hours in the water, we decided to swim to the nearest islands."

Patty, who led multiple rescue efforts, followed with brief remarks about "seeing how fragile humans are and how precious life is, and everybody has to do what they love and be with who they love. The people that died out there loved where they were and they loved what they were doing, and they gave their lives for it."

With that, the three of them departed, and Neal and I remained to answer reporters' questions as best we could. I especially wanted to share other stories of heroism I'd heard earlier in the day—of Professor Nakano's early efforts to pull people back and give them a handhold on the overturned boat, of Becca's continual encouragement of Sarah as they swam to a nearby island after enduring several hours in 65 degree water.

COAST GUARD REPORT

I knew from what Sarah had told me that Becca had truly saved her life, but I had no idea of the dimension of Becca's heroism until the final U.S. Coast Guard report was released to us a few years later. In fact, the Coast Guard had recommended that both Becca and Patty be recognized with awards for their "rescue and lifesaving accomplishments"—Patty for leading several efforts that ultimately resulted in the rescue of the four survivors on two islands and Becca for several acts of heroism.

Our campus community gathered in Freeborn Hall to mourn but also to celebrate the five lives lost in the Sea of Cortez. (Photo: Neil Michel/Axiom)

The Coast Guard's report provides detail about the accident (and about Becca's valor) though names (except for those who died) were generally redacted. But based on media reports at the time and on statements from survivors, it's not terribly hard to understand the report's fuller narrative.

According to the Coast Guard's brief summary of the accident, within the first two hours of the boat's capsizing, "two members [Ralph Haygood and Gary Huxel] were washed away from the vessel and eventually swam to islands in the bay; Polis and another team member [Takuya Abe] died and washed away from the vessel. Later, as the vessel drifted near some islands, two members [Becca Lewison and Sarah Ratay] swam for shore while the remaining three members [Michael Rose, Masahiko Higashi and Shigeru Nakano] stayed with the boat. Four were rescued the following morning from the islands they swam to. The boat and the bodies of four persons were recovered. One person remains missing." The cause of death was noted as head injuries (likely caused by waves slamming them into the boat's hull) and drowning, with an "unspecified chest ailment" also contributing to Gary Polis' death.

Survivor Gary Huxel shared memories of Gary Polis and Michael Rose at the April 10, 2000, memorial. Seated (from left): UC Regent John Davies, Dean Neal Van Alfen and Professor Alan Hastings. (Photo: The Davis Enterprise)

The four survivors all suffered multiple bruises and abrasions.

From that report, we learned that Becca retrieved a flotation device that had drifted away from the capsized boat, showed a survivor who was having a hard time holding onto the boat how to secure a flotation device under each of his arms, tried several times to reposition another's flotation device from his back to his front, after several hours in the cold water advised the four who remained clinging to the drifting boat that their best chance was to swim to a nearby island, encouraged Sarah throughout that 30-45 minute swim, a half-hour later swam out against the current to bring Ralph to shore as he drifted by the island, for 90 minutes waved Ralph's red jacket from the base of the island's lighthouse in hopes of attracting rescuers' attention before nightfall, and found a cave for their overnight shelter.

From the report, we also learned that one of our expedition undergraduates changed boats just before the fateful accident and thus made it safely back to port; that the Japanese researchers were not able swimmers (though Professor Nakano was reportedly a superb diver); and that Becca, once she'd reached the island, thought she'd seen Professor Nakano begin to swim away from the boat, still far out in the current. At that point, all must have been lost for his Kyoto colleague, Professor Higashi, and for Michael Rose. "I know from personal experience during grueling and difficult field research in the mountains of Japan and Montana that [Nakano] never would have left his friends to save himself," said Nakano's Colorado State University colleague Kurt Fausch at our memorial service two weeks later.

Family and friends gathered in the UC Davis Arboretum on Oct. 17, 2001, to dedicate an engraved limestone marker and five symbolic trees in remembrance of the five research- ers who died in the Sea of Cortez. (Photo: Debbie Aldridge/UC Davis)

COMMEMORATING FIVE LIVES

Some 400 members of the campus community gathered in Freeborn Hall at 4 p.m. April 10 to mourn and to console, to remember and ultimately to celebrate the lives of the five gifted scientists who perished in the Sea of Cortez, leaving 11 children without fathers and making widows of five wives.

We opened our arms to Gary Polis' wife, Sharon, and their children Evan, 10, and Maia, 4, and his parents Sam and Marie; Michael Rose's wife, Susan, and her mother, Carol, and stepfather, David; Michael's mother, Lynne; his father, David, and stepmother, Cher- yl; and his sisters, Janna and Shayla. The families of Takuya Abe, Masahiko Higashi and Shigeru Nakano—each of whom left a wife and three children—were unable to attend. We sent flowers to the memorial services in Japan, conveying our deepest sympathies to the bereaved families and to the Kyoto University community.

"We are not used to losing our colleagues in this way," Neal Van Alfen said at our campus memorial. "When tragedy was thrust on these people, they responded with heroism and honor. I have been a close spectator as the survivors have told their stories and have been overwhelmed by the accounts of the grief, valor and courage of those who were struck by this tragedy. I've heard tales of real heroes, including some who lost their lives."

The three Kyoto University ecologists—whose loss particularly dealt a blow to the field of termite biology—were remembered by Nobuaki Tanaka, the Consul General of the San Francisco Japanese Consulate. The Consul General said that, when he first arrived in San Francisco, he paid tribute at the graves of three Japanese sailors who long ago died in

Dean Neal Van Alfen spoke of the grove's significance as a living memorial. (Photo: Debbie Aldridge/UC Davis)

their country's first attempt to cross the Pacific Ocean in order to establish Japan's first U.S. embassy. "These young men from Kyoto University reminded me of these brave soldiers 140 years ago—all of them zealous, adventurous and also hopeful.... Perhaps the only difference then and now is that this time they are on the same boat with the Americans. Japan and the U.S. share the joy as well as the sorrow."

Survivor Gary Huxel recalled Gary Polis' pure joy during a previous expedition as a whale spouted just 10 meters off the boat. "He had the broadest smile. He was beaming being able to share this experience with us, knowing Baja would change our lives forever. He put his hand on my shoulder and said, 'This is how I want to be remembered.'"

Clutching the podium and struggling not to break down, Gary next offered his remembrance of Michael Rose, "a friend I knew I'd have for life.... I'll remember Michael with a smile on his face, mischief in his heart, honesty, humility, integrity, kindness, compassion, joy, wonderment and love in his soul."

Others shared memories and condolences. The UCD Symphony Orchestra and Chorus performed moving selections from Mozart and Bach. And the Gospel Choir sang the stirring yet soothing anthem "Speak to My Heart."

I concluded the memorial by announcing that the campus would honor the memories of Gary Allan Polis, Michael David Rose, Takuya Abe, Masahiko Higashi and Shigeru Nakano with a memorial planting of trees—"each to stand sturdy, reaching to the sky and its 'matrix of millions of pinpoint stars' about which Michael Rose wrote and [that] so inspired him and his fellow expeditioners. We have been privileged to know them. They will be sorely missed."

A LIVING MEMORIAL

Family, friends and colleagues gathered in the UC Davis Arboretum on Oct. 17, 2001, for the dedication of an engraved limestone marker and five symbolic trees in remembrance of Gary, Michael and Professors Abe, Higashi and Nakano.

The marker, engraved in both English and Japanese, includes this quote (one of Gary Polis' favorites) from John Steinbeck's *Sea of Cortez*: "Life and living: Lord, how the day passes! It is like a life, so quickly when we don't watch it, and so slowly if we do."

"Trees are living memorials," Neal Van Alfen said at the gathering. "They grow and change, and we can think of what might have been if (the researchers) were still with us."

Gary's wife, Sharon, and Michael's wife, Susan, also spoke, offering remembrances and thanks.

Unfortunately, the wives of the three Japanese scientists—Yayoi Abe, Tomoko Higashi and Hiromi Nakano—and Kyoto University President Nagao Makoto were not able to attend, each sending their regrets and expressing their hope to visit in the future. As Tomoko wrote to me, "The growth of trees will give us a strength and an energy to live as a memory of my husband's life forever."

On the 10th anniversary of its planting, the memorial grove had grown and changed. With me that day were International Programs Vice Provost Bill Lacy (center) and Assistant Vice Provost Bob Kerr (right). (Photo: Maril Stratton/UC Davis)

I asked Professor Charles Goldman, who was traveling to Japan a few weeks later, to hand-carry to President Nagao videotapes of the memorial tree dedication, along with written translations of the words of our speakers, photographs and printed copies of the memorial plaque (for the widows as well as for Kyoto University). Charles met with the president and Norio Yamamura, director of the university's Center for Ecological Research, on Nov. 16, for what he described as a "very cordial, somewhat emotional hour of tea" where the video was viewed and the materials examined with care. Center director Yamamura later wrote to me that "the [tree dedication] ceremony was very moving, and we were touched by the speeches of colleagues and families of victims of the accident.... We felt your sympathy in honoring and sharing the memory of our colleagues, Drs. Abe, Higashi and Nakano."

"We felt your sympathy in honoring and sharing the memory of our colleagues, Drs. Abe, Higashi and Nakano."

—Norio Yamamura, director of Kyoto University's Center for Ecological Research

I would visit with Yayoi Abe and Tomoko Higashi (Hiromi Nakano was not able to join us) in Kyoto on March 19, 2002, again expressing condolences. Yayoi and Tomoko gave me a book (*Biodiversity: An Ecological Perspective*) edited by their husbands, and I gave them each a porcelain figurine of a California bird and flower (and left one to be given later to Hiromi).

We corresponded again on the 10th anniversary of the memorial grove's planting. I'd wanted to show them through recent photographs how the grove had grown, and to let them know that they were still in our thoughts. Through their responses, I learned of children growing and thriving (some pursuing science just as their fathers had), of memories held close to their hearts, of the belief that a husband continues to watch over and protect his family from heaven. And I learned that Takuya and Yayoi's eldest son (now a mathematician) had had the opportunity to visit the grove in 2009 while attending a seminar at UC Davis. I hope he felt some comfort there. His father—like Masahiko Higashi, Shigeru Nakano, Gary Polis and Michael Rose—continues to live in the memories and hearts of those left behind, memorialized in a particularly beautiful and contemplative area of our Arboretum.

I hope—for all the families—that time has helped turn grief to peace. That would bring me comfort.

▶ **http://escholarship.org/uc/ucdavischancelloremeritus_books**

Surviving Tragedy

Nearly a decade and a half later, I'm struck by the resilience of the tragedy's four survivors.

Becca Lewison went on to complete her doctorate in ecology at UC Davis and, at this writing, holds a faculty position at San Diego State University where she heads a research group studying the impact of resource and land use on vulnerable wildlife populations in both terrestrial and marine environments.

Gary Huxel went on to faculty positions at the University of South Florida and the University of Arkansas, consults on environmental and ecological issues and, at this writing, is completing a master's degree in environmental law through the Vermont Law School, focusing on climate change and energy policy.

Sarah Ratay completed her bachelor's degree in plant biology, evolution and ecology at UC Davis, and went on to pursue a Ph.D. in ecology and evolutionary biology at UCLA and to serve as a Catalina Island Conservancy plant ecologist.

And Ralph Haygood completed his doctorate in population biology at UC Davis and went on to post-doc fellowships at the University of Wisconsin, Madison, and at Duke University. He describes himself as a scientist (studying evolution, ecology, genetics and genomics) and an entrepreneur (founding a virtual business card company and developing software for managing and analyzing DNA samples). His Web page includes an acknowledgment of his having survived the boating accident: "I could easily have died too, but with help from another survivor, I got to shore. I'd never been much of an aquatic animal, and now I'm even less so."

They've survived the sea and the trauma that surely followed. For that, I'm immensely grateful.

Five Remarkable Lives

Excerpts from the printed program of the April 10, 2000, celebration of the lives of Gary Allan Polis, Michael David Rose, Takuya Abe, Masahiko Higashi and Shigeru Nakano:

GARY ALLAN POLIS

"A feisty, energetic, original thinker" … "a gift for bringing people together"

An internationally renowned scorpion expert and ecologist, Gary Allan Polis, 53, chaired and taught in UC Davis' Department of Environmental Science and Policy. Gary was relatively new to the campus, arriving in 1998, six years after he and his family spent a sabbatical leave here, and after teaching nearly 20 years at Vanderbilt University. He grew up in California, earning his bachelor's degree at Loyola University, and his M.A. and Ph.D. degrees at UC Riverside. His scholarship focused on scorpions and food web ecology. He authored *Biology of Scorpions*, *The Ecology of Desert Communities* and, in press, *Scorpions Biology and Research*, and co-authored *Scorpion Man: Exploring the World of Scorpions*. He often traveled to the islands of Baja California for research, at times taking his wife, Sharon, and children, Evan and Maia. Gary's interest in sharing his scientific knowledge extended well beyond the academic world to broader audiences—National Geographic films and PBS documentaries featured him. His professional achievements included presiding over the American Society of Naturalists, serving as an Aldo Leopold Leadership Fellow and receiving, in 1992, a Fulbright fellowship for research.

MICHAEL DAVID ROSE

"Kind, gentle and always optimistic" … "always had a smile on his face"

Born in California, Michael David Rose, 27, grew up in Lebanon, Illinois. He earned his bachelor's degree in biology from Vanderbilt University, and his master's degree in behavioral ecology from Northern Arizona University. As a graduate student, he taught and conducted research on ecological systems, publishing his findings in *Ecology* and other journals. In graduate school, he was a mentor with the National Science Foundation Young Scholars Program, training students and teachers in biological principles and research techniques. Michael and his wife, Susan, married in 1995. The couple moved to Davis in the late 1990s. Michael worked for Professor Gary Polis as a postgraduate researcher in the UC Davis Department of Environmental Science and Policy. Michael conducted research and coordinated a research program with the Earthwatch Institute. He found the mystique of the Baja California landscape to be contagious. Combining his passion for nature, travel and writing, he was in the process of drafting a travel guide about Baja California.

TAKUYA ABE

"A true gentleman, a quiet man" … "the consummate field ecologist"

Takuya Abe, 55, was a professor of animal ecology at the Center for Ecological Research at Kyoto University in Japan. He was an expert on termite biology and the role termites play in ecosystems, and was noted for discovering patterns in the ways different termite species nest and use resources.

MASAHIKO HIGASHI

"A scientist with an artist's sensibility" … "despite his clearly superior abilities, he was unfailingly humble"

Masahiko Higashi, 45, was a theoretical ecologist at the Center for Ecological Research. He was considered the premier theoretical ecologist and biologist in Japan. He had developed several models on such topics as sexual selection and food webs and the evolution of social structure. He collaborated often with Takuya Abe; together they developed a landmark theory of the evolution of social behavior in termites.

SHIGERU NAKANO

"An incredible ecologist" … "an uncommonly genuine person"

Shigeru Nakano, 37, was a community ecologist at the Center for Ecological Research. His interest in food webs took him to streams and forests around the world, including Japan, Borneo and North America, where he worked to understand the interaction of land- and water-based food chains.

When Winning Is Losing

Inevitably as college sport becomes financially dependent on winning, ugly things begin to happen. We must not go there.
—THEN-ASSOCIATE VICE CHANCELLOR BOB FRANKS IN NOVEMBER 2001 ABOUT A POTENTIAL MOVE TO DIVISION I ATHLETICS

WE COULDN'T STAY WHERE WE WERE. THERE WASN'T ANY "THERE" THERE ANYMORE.

Our National Collegiate Athletic Association Division II intercollegiate athletics conference was crumbling as members defected or dropped sports. We were competing with schools a fraction of our size. And our game schedules paired us with institutions that were far from our academic peers.

I announced our D-I intentions at a March 2003 news conference, flanked by Donald DeRosa, University of the Pacific president and Big West Conference immediate past president; Dennis Farrell, Big West Conference commissioner; and Greg Warzecka, UC Davis athletics director. (Photo: Debbie Aldridge/UC Davis)

The landscape was rapidly shifting in 2002 and we needed to find firmer ground, and find it fast. There was too much at stake. We knew we couldn't stand still if we were to preserve and improve what we had—an athletic program truly centered on the student-athlete and the teacher-coach, and integrated with (and accountable to) an academic program.

We were seeking an "Ivy League of the West" kind of affiliation—where recruited athletes measured up academically to the rest of their classmates and where participation in athletics was viewed as an important part of a well-rounded education.

The Big West Conference fit the bill. The fact it was Division I was almost incidental. Most importantly, it was a group of universities very much like ourselves—including our sister campuses of UC Irvine, UC Riverside and UC Santa Barbara—and with our academic values. And the conference was looking for another institution just like ours. It couldn't have been a better fit, and the invitation to join couldn't have come at a better time.

We stunned Stanford 20-17 in a thrilling 2005 come-from-behind upset, but we shouldn't expect to routinely take down teams a subdivision higher. (Photo: UC Davis)

"BIG TIME" COLLEGE SPORTS

To be clear, we were never aiming for the Pac-12—for Division I "big time" athletics. Nor were we looking to abandon our educational model of athletics in favor of a "business" model with its emphasis on sports as revenue-generating, headline-making entertainment. I'd seen firsthand the dangers of this athletic model at the University of Wisconsin, Purdue University, the University of Illinois, and the University of Maryland and knew we didn't want to go there.

You know the all-too-familiar litany of concerns about big-time college sports: the insatiable drive to win, softened admissions standards and abysmal graduation rates for athletes, bogus classes, skyrocketing compensation for coaches and staff, diversion of funds from academic programs (only a handful of these D-I programs break even), growing commercialization of sports, and an athletics culture in open conflict with the university's educational principles and values.

"Big-time college sports do far more damage to the university—its students and faculty, its leadership, and its reputation and credibility—than most people realize or are willing to admit," wrote University of Michigan President Emeritus Jim Duderstadt in his 2007 book *The View from the Helm.*

Surely that's a view shared by the presidents of universities associated with the more recent spate of sports scandals (for example, Penn State, Ohio State, the University of Miami, the University of North Carolina, the University of Oregon, the University of Montana, Rutgers, UC Berkeley, Syracuse—the list is long and growing).

It didn't surprise me to see Holden Thorp (the University of North Carolina's departing chancellor who headed to Washington University in St. Louis in July 2013 to become its provost) announce his relief to be trading in a perennial NCAA Division I national championship contender for a school that plays at the NCAA's lowest division. For two years, he'd been dogged by problems in UNC-Chapel Hill's athletics program. That's not how any university president hopes to be spending his or her time.

As I'd told *The NCAA News* in October 2004, "I knew that if we continued to take only the very best students—which means that we wouldn't be selecting simply for the very best athletes—that in turn we probably wouldn't be going to the Rose Bowl. I'm right there in front of the TV when March Madness is going on, but I've never envied those universities, presidents or coaches. It's the kind of pressure that puts all of the emphasis on athletics and just not enough on what universities are all about."

Athletics Director Greg Warzecka introduced scholarships for student-athletes and guided our transition to Division I.

"THE DAVIS WAY" CORE PRINCIPLES

So how could we keep the emphasis where it needed to be? What was to prevent our sliding down the slippery slope of big-time D-I athletics when we joined the Big West Conference?

Principles—a set of core principles that codified and safeguarded "the Davis Way," that made a promise to undergraduates who'd approved a Division I-enabling student-fee initiative, and that assured our campus community our athletics program would maintain its integrity and remain student-centered and academically focused.

Those principles were largely the work of Bob Franks, then associate vice chancellor for student affairs and a key player in our deliberations. For more than 23 years, he'd been adamantly opposed to the D-I idea. But the possibility of affiliation with the Big West when our D-II conference was collapsing turned him from critic to advocate—provided we could structurally engineer safeguards against any worrisome consequences.

Bob Franks, associate vice chancellor for student affairs, espoused a principled approach to Division I athletics.

The eight principles were our safeguards, intended to

ensure our "Davis Way" philosophy continued to provide the foundation for our athletics programs long after we'd left our administrative positions.

Even so, our faculty were worried—and that worried Bob. I clearly remember when he came to my office very concerned that the Academic Senate planned to vote on the issue. I didn't improve his state of mind. "It's worse than you think," I'd told him. "The vote will likely be two to one against the move, despite all your work to make sure our athletics program continues to walk the high road."

And sure enough, the faculty nixed a move to D-I in an advisory vote of 556 to 271 in February 2003. But an Academic Senate committee that studied the move's budget implications concluded that the student fee-funded model "is thought to provide the best opportunity for maintaining or perhaps enhancing the current 'student scholar-athlete' culture of the current program because it is student-funded and the financial success of the programs will not be dependent on the win-loss record of the teams and the majority of the program will not be dependent on the vagaries of the campus budget situation." It recommended pegging grants-in-aid funding to team academic performance, rewarding teams with strong grade point averages and graduation rates and penalizing those that fall short.

A second senate committee studied the academic implications of a D-I move, finding that many faculty had "confused potential membership in Division I-A [now the Football Bowl Subdivision] with actual membership in Division I-AA [now the Football Championship Subdivision]." The distinction is important, it said, since most DI-AA programs are strongly connected to the academic mission and have smaller, non-self-supporting budgets. "It is clear that the current athletic program is one of high quality in terms of academic integrity, and that it fits well with the overall mission of the campus," the committee wrote. "We do not see the transition to Division I-AA jeopardizing that position."

Undergrads celebrate the 2002 passage of a student fee initiative that made D-I athletics possible. Pictured are Jennifer (Wong) Wade, Lisa (Wade) Wells and Gregory Ortiz, all now UC Davis staff members. (Photo: The Davis Enterprise)

Others weighed in, as well: undergraduates, approving the fee initiative 4,638 to 3,929; the Student-Athlete Advisory Committee, voting 38 to 1 in favor; and the Athletic Administrative Advisory Committee (which included faculty and students), voting 11-2, with one abstention, in favor. I also weighed carefully the views of

Before a crowd of nearly 10,000 on Sept. 1, 2007, Western Washington upset UC Davis 28-21 in the first football game played at Aggie Stadium. Temperatures soared over 100 degrees, with 85 fans treated for heat-related problems and eight transported to area hospitals, none in serious condition. Lights were added the next season so game starts could shift to late afternoon/early evening. (Photo: Cheng Saechao/UC Davis)

our longtime teacher-coaches, who built and espoused the virtues of Division II athletics but had come to know we could not preserve what we had if we stood still.

So on March 11, 2003, we declared our intention to join the Big West Conference and began our transition to Division I.

We believed we could do it right and, in the process, continue to be a national model. But did we? And are we?

I'm not so sure.

"BIG-TIME" WORRIES

Our core principles—meant to guide our behavior far into the future—won't necessarily guarantee it. Our 2006 NCAA "Certification of Self-Study Report" noted that any "departures from or changes to the eight core campus principles guiding intercollegiate athletics" would require special review beyond the athletics program—all the way to the chancellor after he or she had first consulted with the Council of Deans and Vice Chancellors. That provision, while indicating that there may be a legitimate reason over time to reexamine the principles, was primarily intended to provide an extra layer of protection.

I worry that already we may be digressing from the most fundamental of our core principles.

I've been troubled, for example, by the withdrawal of campus general funds for teacher-coach-taught Physical Education classes from the athletics budget. Those funds have paid the lecturer portion of our teacher-coach salaries, which I believe, on principle, should not be supported by student fees or other Intercollegiate Athletics funds. And, not insignificantly, that unexpected $2 million budget cut to ICA led to the elimination of four sports in 2010. That's not to say that ICA should be shielded when budgets are being slashed across the campus, but this special additional cut—with very short notice—left little room for Athletics Director Greg Warzecka to respond. And it upended our longstanding policy that state funds—not student fees—should pay for courses with academic credit.

I'm also concerned about the suggestion that our new coaches should focus solely on their teams and no longer be expected to additionally teach PE courses. Our teacher-coach model has long kept our coaches connected to the academic community and to the general student body—not just to elite athletes in individual sports.

I winced, as well, to see Chancellor Linda Katehi's Oct. 5, 2011, appointment letter to the Director of Athletics search committee. In it, she'd referenced an audit she'd commissioned from former NCAA president Cedric Dempsey: "I believe Division I is the right fit for UC Davis now and for the future. However, as the strategic audit indicates, the eight principles that were outlined and adopted during our transition to Division I do not appear to align with a successful Division I athletics program in today's environment: indeed, consultant Cedric Dempsey writes in his report that the majority of these principles 'represent an impediment to increased competitiveness in Division I.'

Sports Illustrated *twice named UC Davis the best NCAA Division II school for women athletes. Twenty-three varsity sports are currently offered—14 women's and nine men's teams. (Photo: UC Davis)*

The consultant recommends among other things that UC Davis 'evaluate and adjust the eight (8) principles to more closely coincide with NCAA Division I' philosophies and practices. A careful and thoughtful review of these principles is one of the report's many recommendations that I urge you to consider, all with an eye toward helping to define a vision of excellence for our athletics program for today and tomorrow…. This will then allow for the hiring of a Director of Athletics who will design a strategic plan that will help guide us toward a new level of excellence."

I shouldn't have been surprised by that challenge to our "inviolate" principles. In that same 2004 *The NCAA News* article, then-NCAA Division I Board of Directors Chair and University of Kansas Chancellor Robert Hemenway noted, "How often have you heard people say they've hired a new coach or president and he or she is going to take them to another level? It's almost as if we have a template built into our heads that the next level is always better than the level we're on."

> **"I voted for D-I, but I don't believe in the business model. I want us to be the best of the best but not at the cost of my integrity."**
>
> **—Faculty member at October 2011 town hall**

But, to Linda's credit, she directed the athletics director search committee to hold town hall meetings to gather advice on the best future direction for our athletics program. I was heartened by the passionate affirmation of our "Davis Way" philosophy by so many of the faculty, students, staff, alumni and parents who attended. "I voted for D-I, but I don't believe in the business model. I want us to be the best of the best but not at the cost of my integrity." "Double-down on our model. It's better; it just happens to be rare." "Emulate Stanford, not LSU." "We can improve, but there's a lot we have to preserve." "Reject the notion we should look to others. Let us lead, not follow."

The search committee listened, and advised the chancellor that academic integrity should remain ICA's highest priority and that an understanding of what athletics "success" and "excellence" mean needed to be reached.

Linda listened, too, reiterating the search committee's recommendations in her response—but prompting this Jan. 10, 2012, *California Aggie* editorial in the process: "During October and November it looked almost certain that the university would be hiring a big-time athletic director, and UC Davis would be following the recommendations for sweeping change made by the Dempsey Report—possibly including the cutting of sports. But Friday, Katehi released a letter stating that she has no intention of making major changes to UC Davis athletics. We may never know the true motivation behind Katehi's statement. Maybe she was swayed by the strongly anti-Dempsey Report sentiment expressed at each of the four town hall meetings. Maybe she was truly convinced that UC Davis could not support a major sports program. Regardless, the immediate reaction of many was that Katehi's decision was based on a post-pepper spray desire to avoid another controversy, like the one seen when four sports were cut in 2010. While we have publicly opposed the cutting of sports by a new athletic director, we also believe it is important for the UC Davis administration to not only make the right choice, but to make it for the right reasons. Judgments that affect the lives of UC Davis students need to be made based on logic and reason, not a fear of controversy."

Whatever the reason, I'm glad for the pullback. And I'm reassured to hear new athletics director Terry Tumey (who now reports directly to the chancellor rather than to the vice chancellor for student affairs) frequently affirm the importance of our student-athletes' success in the classroom as well as on the field or court.

I'd feel even more reassured, though, if his contract had also included incentive pay for student-athlete academic achievements—not just for winning conference championships and qualifying for NCAA tournaments.

"To be a D-I school that focuses as much on academics and the 'teaching' of student-athletes (vs. merely coaching them for a sport), we need to align reward structures with those values," says Kimberly Elsbach, professor of organizational behavior and our faculty athletics representative to the NCAA during our D-I transition. "There is no stronger signal about what an organization values than what it rewards."

The hall talk in the athletics department also suggests a heightened focus on winning.

Coaches with less than a .500 winning average are reportedly worrying, particularly after the 2013 release of a long-time teacher-coach who excelled in teaching and in encouraging his student-athletes' academic success. His team slipped below .500 in 2012-13 despite his overall winning record across 12 seasons. Since then, other coaches with more losses than wins at the end of a season have also departed.

Winning is a worthy goal when it pushes you to become better. But it's corrosive when you're pressured to win, when it no longer matters how you win or who you become in order to notch another victory. That's never been UC Davis. That's not our brand of "Aggie Pride."

Our faculty have flagged another potential worry—compromised admission standards for student-athletes. The percentage of student-athletes admitted by exception to UC eligibility requirements is growing higher than the admit-by-exception percentage in the overall student population. "The intent and expectation is that those percentages should be kept roughly equal," the Academic Senate Special Committee on Athletics stated in its March 2012 report.

Though the numbers are small, there's a noticeable gap between the percentage of our athletes admitted by exception and the percentage of our non-athletes admitted by exception. It grew as large as 14 percent to 3 percent in 2011-12 but improved some in 2012-13, 6 percent to 1 percent. It may simply be a missing Scholastic Aptitude Test score, or a grade point average that doesn't quite meet the higher GPA required of out-of-state students, that accounts for the admission by exception rather than wishful recruiting of a gifted athlete who's likely to struggle academically. In any case, the faculty expect the admit-by-exception percentages for athletes and non-athletes to be kept roughly the same.

Some early departures of student-athletes also suggest that some are coming here first to play a particular sport and, second, to pursue a UC Davis education. That's new for us, too, and worth keeping an eye on—right along with increased spending on high-profile

Admission Characteristics of Incoming Athletes and Non-Athletes at UC Davis
Fall Cohorts, 2003-04 to 2012-13

		Student Type				Grants-In-Aid Athletes		Athletic Participation	
		Non-Athletes		Athletes					
		Count	Percent	Count	Percent	Count	Percent	Count	Percent
Admitted by Exception	2003-04	239	3%	11	5%	7	5%	10	6%
	2004-05	170	3%	12	5%	9	5%	9	4%
	2005-06	177	3%	22	9%	18	12%	16	8%
	2006-07	191	3%	16	7%	10	6%	13	7%
	2007-08	186	3%	10	4%	8	5%	9	5%
	2008-09	136	2%	14	6%	10	5%	12	6%
	2009-10	98	2%	12	5%	10	6%	9	5%
	2010-11	122	2%	19	11%	19	12%	15	10%
	2011-12	200	3%	23	14%	23	15%	17	12%
	2012-13	90	1%	11	6%	7	6%	5	4%

The Academic Senate expects the percentage of student-athletes admitted by exception to UC eligibility requirements to be roughly equal to the ABE percentage in the overall student population. (Source: UC Davis Institutional Analysis—Student Research & Information)

men's sports (for example, for hotel rooms for the football team on the eve of *home* football games) that could make it harder for us to meet our Title IX obligations to provide comparable benefits to women athletes.

TRUE "AGGIE PRIDE"

I hope we'll still be able to tell stories like that of Elliot Vallejo, a highly recruited offensive tackle who found he couldn't combine his academic goal of becoming an engineer with the time constraints of UCLA football. So, in 2003, he transferred to UC Davis, where the coaching staff allowed his class schedule to trump practices and where teammates were equally focused on their education. He was a standout on the field and in the classroom, ultimately playing for the NFL's Arizona Cardinals (all the way to the 2009 Super Bowl) and earning a master's degree in engineering.

And I hope we'll still have thrilling moments like our Sept. 17, 2005, upset of Stanford, when our football team overcame a 17-point deficit to win 20-17 on a late touchdown with just 8 seconds left in the game. It was the second of five Aggie triumphs over the Cardinal that year: men's soccer, men's basketball, wrestling and baseball also posted victories.

But we shouldn't expect to routinely upset teams a subdivision higher. UC Berkeley, for example, trounced us 52-3 in 2010, adding an easy "W" to their win-loss column while providing us a share of their gate receipts in recompense. This is more likely to be our experience with the Football Bowl Subdivision teams as long as we stay where we are—in this Football Championship Subdivision position in between Division II and the highest

In the first official athletics contest at the new stadium, the women's lacrosse team defeated St. Mary's, 17-5, on April 1, 2007. (Photo: Wayne Tilcock/The Davis Enterprise)

levels of Division I. But, in my view, this is exactly where we belong.

We have too much at risk to make ourselves vulnerable to the scandalous behavior that seems to inevitably attach itself to FBS teams and coaches and to their universities.

Our core principles give us our first line of defense. But our faculty will need to keep their eye on the ball—because, as University of Michigan President Emeritus Duderstadt also recognized, it's the faculty who, ultimately, are responsible for the academic integrity of the university.

I'm glad to see they've engaged. The Academic Senate's Special Committee on Athletics in its March 2012 report affirmed our core principles and recommended the addition of "Principle 0" to make explicit some fundamental assumptions of the original eight: "Intercollegiate athletics at UC Davis is a student-centered, academically focused program. Opportunities for participation along with the welfare and accomplishments of student athletes in both academics and athletics are its primary concerns. Benefits to the institution are secondary."

The committee went on to cite the dangers of a "business" model of athletics, to address admissions and budget process shortcomings, and to recommend that all head and assistant coaches hold at least 32 percent time lecturer appointments (funded by the campus, not ICA). And it made several recommendations to strengthen the Senate's oversight of athletics.

This is a good start, but I hope the senate remains suited up. As its special committee noted, "Many people who are committed to the Davis Way and who have made the system work will retire. Pressure to increase the priority of athletic performance relative to academic performance will increase and stress the system."

And, as the NCAA's most elite Division I programs have sadly shown, the risk "game clock" is constantly ticking. In such a circumstance, we can't have our faculty leaders sitting on the bench.

▶ http://escholarship.org/uc/ucdavischancelloremeritus_books

The Costly Influence of Money

It didn't take long—just a few decades—to see the troubling impact of television money on university athletic programs.

In 1960, that future wasn't so clear. In fact, when television first showed interest in buying the rights to broadcast games, universities were relieved to find an outside organization willing to help fund the increasing costs of college athletics.

But by the '80s and '90s, we'd realized that, as a group, we'd given away the store—and a whole lot more. We'd thought we were solving the big problem of funding athletics. Instead, we were generating the first stages of a *truly* big problem.

We'd relinquished control of the TV money to the athletic conferences and their commissioners, who before long were distributing eye-popping sums to college athletic programs—programs backed by a growing contingent of avid alumni and other fans hungering to see their teams play, and win, on national television. And the broadcast industry was willing to pay—big-time. For instance, Turner Broad¬casting and CBS Sports in 2010 signed a 14-year, $10.8 billion television deal for rights to the Division I men's basketball championship. And ESPN has reportedly agreed to pay $7.4 billion over 12 years for the rights to telecast football's new championship system season-capping games—four major bowl games, two semifinal bowl games and the national championship game.

It's elephant-in-the-room clear that universities, and especially university presidents, have lost control as team operating budgets soar, facilities spending spirals, coaches' salaries sharply escalate, and reports of NCAA regulation violations grow.

Nearly 87 percent of college presidents responding to a 2012 *Inside Higher Ed* survey said "they did not believe presidents of institutions with big-time sports programs are in control of those programs." And three-quarters of them acknowledged that "colleges and universities spend way too much money on intercollegiate athletic programs."

The Knight Commission's 2010 *Restoring the Balance: Dollars, Values, and the Future of College Sports* report warned of the "financial arms race [that] threatens the continued viability of athletics programs and the integrity of our universities." The growing focus on winning games "and increasing television market share feeds the spending escalation because of the unfounded yet persistent belief that devoting more dollars to sports programs leads to greater athletic success and thus to greater revenues. In fact, only a tiny number of college athletics programs actually reap the financial rewards that come from selling high-priced tickets and winning championships."

Thankfully, we don't have the capacity—at least not yet—to be a player in this race. It'd take a billion dollar gift for us to generate the funds needed to compete with what consultant Cedric Dempsey calls "the big boys"—those big-time Division I athletic programs whose budgets and facilities dwarf ours. We'd need to add 50,000 seats to Aggie Stadium and 4,000 seats to the basketball pavilion, and many million dollars more to Intercollegiate Athletics' annual operating budget (it's expensive to recruit and support superstar players and coaches).

That's a competition I'm happy to lose.

If universities fail to reform, the Knight Commission predicted an "increased subsidy of athletics programs at the cost of academic programs, higher mandatory athletics fees for all students at many institutions, and a reduction in sports offerings—including dropping

Aggie Stadium, home to the women's lacrosse team and the football team, opened in 2007 and provides about 9,000 fixed seats and 3,000 berm seats. (Photo: Jim von Rummelhoff/UC Davis

of teams that are not generating revenues. Such outcomes are indefensible for an enterprise that exists for the benefit of student participants and should serve to strengthen the academic mission of the university."

The writing on the wall couldn't be clearer.

Eight Principles of The Davis Way*

- **UC Davis must offer a program that does not compromise the University's focus on the academic integrity of student-athletes.**

- **Admissions and graduation standards must in no way be specially altered or amended for athletes.**

- **There can be no "tiering" among UC Davis sports, with some sports and their athletes receiving a better standard of treatment than others.**

- **UC Davis cannot retreat from its Title IX (gender equity) progress but must continue to expand its efforts and compliance.**

- **UC Davis cannot reduce its broad-based program but rather must seek to add sports.**

- **The Athletics program cannot depend for its financial survival on its record of wins and losses.**

- **Permanent core funding must come from students and the institution, rather than from a dependency on external sources.**

- **The athletics department at UC Davis must maintain a formal connection to the mission of the University, including preserving the teacher/coach role.**

adopted by UC Davis in 2003 during the transition from NCAA Division II to Division I

From Old County Hospital to Top-Flight Academic Medical Center

I just jumped up in the air and yelled and yelled when we beat out UCSF and Stanford. That was a great triumph for UC Davis.
—HIBBARD WILLIAMS, SCHOOL OF MEDICINE DEAN EMERITUS

AUDACIOUS. CLEARLY AUDACIOUS—RIGHT FROM THE START.

How could anyone have believed—I mean, really, how could they?—that a run-down county hospital predominantly caring for the Sacramento region's poorest patients could be transformed into a nationally ranked, acute-care academic medical center serving 33 counties and 6 million residents?

The smart money wasn't on us. But we had the visionaries on our side.

UC Davis needed an affiliation with a patient-care facility for our newly created School of Medicine (a framed, soy sauce-stained and legislator-signed slice of a Frank Fat's tablecloth commemorates the sealing of the deal for the school's establishment).

And, in 1966, Sacramento County Hospital was our best bet (though campus folklore suggests that founding dean Dr. John Tupper—a creative, enterprising leader—had also seriously considered the possibility of docking a Navy hospital ship at the Port of Sacramento).

Dr. C. John Tupper, School of Medicine founding dean (Photo: UC Davis)

"Tup" (and Chancellors Emil Mrak and Jim Meyer) knew we had to make the county hospital work—especially after back-to-back failed bond measures dashed our hopes for constructing our own clinical teaching hospital in Davis. To boot, the county, seeing Medi-Cal fiscal troubles brewing, essentially threatened to pull the plug on our affiliation agreement unless we took responsibility for the operation and financing of the hospital.

We were in a bind. Elmer Learn, my predecessor as executive vice chancellor, would joke that he had a full head of hair before engaging in six long years of turbulent negotiations with Sacramento County on ownership and control of the hospital.

After a little head-knocking intervention from the Legislature, a selling price was set: $1 for the hospital, plus $8 million for other buildings, land, equipment and supplies. The university took title on July 1, 1973, but that wasn't the end of our problems—not by a long shot.

Executive Vice Chancellor Elmer Learn (at left and inset), Dean John Tupper and the Sacramento County Board of Supervisors chair signed the agreement transferring the Sacramento Medical Center to UC Davis in 1972. (Photo: UC Davis)

We'd inherited an $11 million mountain of uncollected hospital bills, discovered serious seismic deficiencies in the main building, and still needed to negotiate annual contracts for providing indigent care to county residents. Just as Elmer had predicted, consolidating responsibility for indigent medical care and for teaching and clinical research was not going to be easy.

When the county early on failed to pay its fair share for indigent care, the university served notice to return the hospital. Regents and legislators jumped in, with the county ultimately "agreeing to reimburse us for care we provided on [its] behalf and to an absolute limit on that care because we could see the possibility that we would become totally immersed in care of the needy and that did not provide us with the breadth of experiences that is needed for a good teaching program," Elmer said in a 1995 UC Davis Emeriti Association video interview.

With that benchmark agreement in place, the campus could now concentrate on developing the hospital as a university medical center—as a genuine health sciences campus. On July 1, 1978, the hospital was renamed the University of California, Davis, Medical Center (UCDMC).

Things were looking up, but there would quickly be more storms to weather.

On June 28, 1978, the U.S. Supreme Court had issued its ruling in the Allan Bakke case, finding that "quotas" were illegal but that race could be considered as one factor in admissions. Though the court endorsed continued (though limited) consideration of race, minority applications dropped dramatically as people mistakenly thought affirmative action was dead at UC Davis' School of Medicine.

QUALITY OF CARE CRISIS

And just three years later, shortly after Dr. Hibbard Williams succeeded Tup as dean, a very public dispute over patient outcomes (aggressively covered by a *Sacramento Bee* investigative reporter) erupted between UCDMC cardiologists and surgeons and, soon after, within the med center's renal transplant program. Open heart surgeries and kidney transplants were suspended while the charges were investigated. The state Department of Health Services and the Board of Medical Quality Assurance (BMQA) stepped in, as well as the Joint Commission on Accreditation of Healthcare Organizations (which postponed its renewal of our accreditation). Ultimately, the BMQA cleared the surgeons of all charges, but we'd already undertaken a comprehensive review of our medical care practices.

It was Elmer again who put his finger on a fundamental problem—our medical department chairs had duties beyond those of traditional academic chairs. They must also supervise faculty as medical staff and run an operational entity within the hospital. It became clear to us that we needed to do more to standardize how we ensured appropriate oversight and the highest quality of patient care.

"We developed a whole new system of quality assurance for evaluating patient care and performance of physicians, and for evaluating the performance of hospital departments and how they worked and interacted," Hibbard recalls. "At that point, we actually be-

UC Davis Medical Center, 1978 (Photo: UC Davis)

came a model for other institutions in this country in how to develop a quality assurance program. It was miserable at the time, but we probably wouldn't have improved had it not been for the quality of care crisis that had occurred."

Much of what we'd developed was subsequently adopted by the healthcare accrediting commission—and that changed the national practice of medicine.

STARTING FRESH

By the time I arrived at UC Davis in 1984, that particular dust was beginning to settle. But med center morale was unusually low and the reasons weren't limited to the just-finished, very public bloodbath among the heart docs (with libel, slander and malpractice lawsuits still circling—so much so that UC Office of the President attorneys had had to take an apartment in Sacramento). Additionally, our employees were working in poor facilities; the hospital's financial circumstance was borderline and headed down; community relations were dismal; and there seemed to be no clear understanding of how the med school dean and the hospital director should interact.

As the new executive vice chancellor (and the med center's official "Governing Body"), I had to get up to speed pronto on the health sciences. The hospital director, the medical director, the School of Medicine dean and the hospital itself (through the dean and director) all reported directly to me.

Hibbard Williams, second dean of the School of Medicine (Photo: UC Davis)

Quite by accident, we had an entirely new team of leaders and that team had the right combination of talents: Dr. Hibbard Williams, dean; Frank Loge, newly named hospital director; and Dr. Joe Tupin, the newly appointed medical director. We also had just hired or advanced several key people just a step or two down who would become stars: Mike Boyd in facility services; Carol Robinson in nursing administration; and Geneva Harris in clinical affairs. And we had many new young clinical chairs—faculty like Drs. Michael Chapman, Rick Chole, Faith Fitzgerald, Robert Hale, Joe Silva (who would eventually become dean), Dennis Styne, Franklin Wagner and Ralph deVere White)—who would go on to head up centers, rejuvenate tired departments and describe for their faculty how a top-notch medical facility should be behaving.

Hibbard, Frank, Joe and I agreed on four basic principles. First, no surprises—we all needed to be aware of all new developments. Second, neither the dean nor the director could proceed independently on a project that affected the other; I would be the tie-breaker if they couldn't agree. Third, unless absolutely impossible, our docs must practice in our facilities; they couldn't walk both sides of the university/private practice street. And fourth—and most importantly—academic mission must always come first; that's where planning had to begin.

We agreed, as well, that we needed to stop spending all our time putting out grass fires. We had to begin to plan for the long term. We first needed a School of Medicine academic plan. Then we needed a UCDMC strategic plan that laid out the specific ways the med center would support the school's academic plan, meet service obligations to the community and maintain financial viability. Next, we needed a UCDMC Long-Range Development Plan and, finally, an LRDP financial plan.

Joined by a few others, we met monthly as the Joint Management Council. As chair, I insisted that there would be no flimflam allowed at these meetings; here, we needed to be our own toughest critics. I also informally visited the hospital unannounced. Sitting in the waiting rooms gave me insight from the patient's perspective. Visiting the emergency room on a Friday night helped me understand the trauma of treating trauma cases—something that was very important to our ER physicians and nurses for me to observe. I saw, too, the crisis periods when our ER was overwhelmed and needed to divert ambulances to other hospitals.

We had an enormous responsibility, but we knew what we had to do, and off we went.

MED CENTER VISIONING

No one went off with more confidence or more derring-do than hospital director Frank Loge.

Mike Boyd, executive director of facilities services, remembers that first planning retreat: "The conversation started with 'Well, what is the vision for this place?' Frank, never timid, got up and said, 'Well, I think we need to be big. I'm not sure what it is, but it's big. We need to have big goals and we need to stretch.'"

It was always full steam ahead with Frank, Mike remembers. "He would say if we're going to go down, we're going to go down in flames. We're going to go down big."

And so they started to lay out some audacious goals for the med center—for example, to grow from 900,000 square feet to 3.7 million, from 65 acres to 144. "Can you imagine? He was a visionary."

Bonnie Hyatt, now-retired public affairs director for the hospital, agrees Frank was a transformative force for the medical center. "He had a clear vision, he got his team to share it, and he was relentless in pursuing it."

Formerly the hospital's finance director, Frank found ways—end runs, some would say—to fund what he felt the school and the med center (a tub on its own bottom) needed to have, once even going toe to toe with ABC News' Sam Donaldson in defense of hospital rates.

Early on, he recognized we needed to buy up surrounding property—including 88 homes and the remainder of the old fairgrounds—for research and clinical facilities (prompting an irritated reminder from business and finance vice chancellor Jim Sullivan that "we're in the business of education, not real estate"). Frank quietly began purchasing those homes, hoping sales prices wouldn't skyrocket once it got around that the university was the buyer. Inevitably they did, with asking prices nearly 50 percent higher than when we'd started out. Even so, Frank feared the last neighbor—who ran a dog-boarding facility—wouldn't sell, no matter the price. She held out till the very end.

"I was afraid we were going to have to use eminent domain," Frank recalled in a 2013 UC Davis Emeriti Association video interview. "But one of my colleagues said, 'You know, why don't we go buy her a dog boarding place?' That was a great idea. We found one just a little bit out of town. So we made a deal with her. We painted it. We fixed all the kennels. We helped move all her dogs. She moved happily."

Hospital director Frank Loge guided the development of a 20-year Long-Range Development Plan for the med center. (Photo: UC Davis)

With needed new property secured, building began in earnest. Steam lines were torn out and a more energy-efficient co-generation power plant constructed. The road structure was laid, the information systems and data processing services established, the financial system reorganized, the fundamental foundation formed.

Research and clinical facilities quickly followed.

CREATIVE FINANCING

Hibbard needed medical school research buildings near the hospital for his faculty but didn't yet have enough clinical-practice-plan funding to start construction. Frank knew that patient care dollars couldn't be used for research space, but he saw a way the hospital could get the shovels turning—by loaning the school the funds "at a reasonable interest rate of 0.1 percent…. Through creative financing, without violating or stepping on the rules, we were able to bend them a bit and make a lot of things happen out there"—including providing Hibbard with needed funds to recruit and support superb department chairs and to keep clinical equipment current.

It was Frank's turn to borrow money for the new patient Tower in the early 1990s. The university didn't have sufficient funds to spare, so he devised a plan to borrow against the med center's revenues—an unheard-of approach at the time. The Office of the President—the sole borrowing agent for all of UC—wouldn't guarantee payment of our bonds but eventually agreed to let us guarantee our own if we could convince a New York bond house.

"We actually went to New York and made presentations to a number of large bond houses," Frank said. "We got our money, and paid it off through our own revenue stream, with it clear the University of California had stamped right there: 'We're not backing.' We were able to [win financing] because we had a great, solid track record."

That strong reputation remains a great satisfaction for Frank.

"Of all the old county hospitals the university owns [in Sacramento, San Diego and Irvine], we're the only one, from the day I became director to today, that has never had an operating deficit," Frank said in that 2013 video interview. "[UCDMC] has been able to sustain itself and that's not true of the others."

Staying in the black—just staying afloat—was no easy feat (especially as the practice of medicine shifted to a corporate model, challenging all hospitals—not just academic medical centers—to adapt or go under).

"We did what we had to do and went ahead and made the financial decisions we had to make, and I did a lot of apologizing," Frank said. "…I had a regent once tell me, 'Your toes, all ten, are over the cliff. It's just a matter of time before you fall off, right?'"

SMART INVESTMENTS

Early on, we looked for mission-matching financial winners we could enhance or pursue. Our emerging trauma and emergency services program (led by Dr. Bill Blaisdell, widely regarded as the father of modern trauma surgery) topped the list. It was absolutely transformative, carving out a distinctive niche for UCDMC as (still) the only Level 1 trauma center for both adult and pediatric emergencies in inland Northern California. And it gave our revenues a much-needed boost while solidifying our reputation as the go-to place for the highest quality, most complex critical care.

But we needed a larger and more medically diverse base of patients—particularly as managed care became the medical practice model. So we began recruiting physician practices in a dozen Northern California communities, paving the way for UCDMC's 1995 transition to the UC Davis Health System (comprising our medical faculty, the teaching hospital and the affiliated primary care physicians).

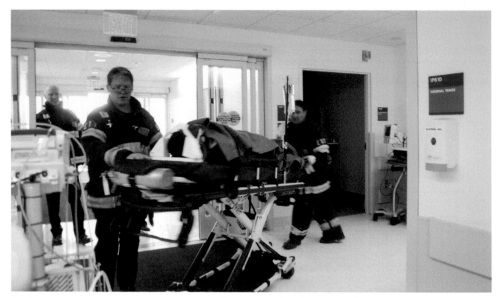

Early on, our trauma program carved out a distinctive niche for UCDMC. (Photo: UC Davis)

At about the same time, Dr. Tom Nesbitt was pioneering another of our signature programs—telemedicine (today one of the largest such programs in the country). Through the Internet, computer monitors and small cameras, Tom had figured out in 1992 how to connect our expert physicians to patients living in remote (primarily rural) communities without access to life-saving, complex specialty care.

Making that connection was crucial, he reminded UC Regents in a 2007 presentation. "If we discover the cure for cancer, but only half the people have access to it, did we discover the cure? Or only half of the cure?"

Through telemedicine, Tom enabled our specialty docs to collaborate, in real time, with small-community physicians, to see and hear and help stabilize patients, to view X-rays, to hear a heartbeat.

I still vividly remember an early visit with Tom to our first telemedicine partner—a hospital in Colusa, a rural town some 60 miles north of Sacramento. We met with three new mothers who, because of telemedicine, had been able to deliver their babies there, in their home community hospital, with their families nearby. That meant the world to them, they tearfully told us. No speeding to a Sacramento delivery room, hoping to outrace their babies' arrival. They could stay home—yet still have the reassuring presence (through telemedicine) of our specialists if birthing complications arose.

Today our telemedicine program links more than 40 medical specialties to over 100 California clinics and hospitals. Our early success in helping to resolve geographic healthcare disparities was expanded and maximized as other UC medical centers jumped in, adding to a robust web of telehealth partners throughout our sprawling state.

That's got to feel satisfying to Tom, though, ever self-effacing, he consistently deflects praise for his pioneering efforts. I was so happy that the regents rewarded him with applause that day in 2007, that California voters had already signaled their support by passing Proposition 1D in 2006, and that Governor Schwarzenegger added his endorsement by subsequently launching the California Telehealth Network.

ABSOLUTELY THRILLING

It'd be hard to find more thrilling moments in UCDHS' history than two announcements—one made in 1990, the other in 2007—that confirmed our standing among the elite academic medical centers and reinforced our reputation as a passionate partner when it came to addressing society's needs.

In 1990, it was the Shriners who gave Dr. Michael Chapman, chair of our Department of Orthopaedics, reason to declare that "this is the most exciting thing that's happened since the founding of the School of Medicine…. [It is] a substantial vote of confidence in the future of UCDMC."

Clearly the underdog, we'd made a compelling—and ultimately convincing—case to the Shriners that they should relocate their Northern California Shriners Hospital for

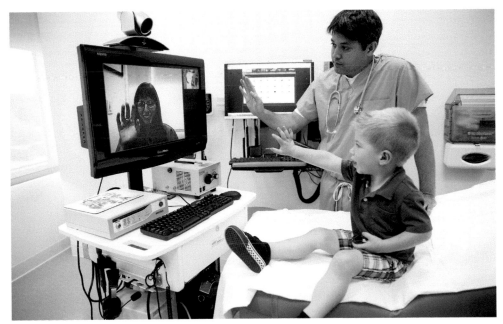

Telemedicine, another signature program, connects our expert physicians to patients living in remote communities without access to specialty care. (Photo: UC Davis)

Shriner leaders, flanked by Dean Hibbard Williams (far left) and Dr. Joe Tupin (far right), in 1990 announced that the Shriners flagship children's hospital would be built adjacent to UCDMC. Stanford and UC San Francisco had also submitted proposals. (Photo: UC Davis)

Children from its San Francisco location to Sacramento, just across the street from our med center on land we had obtained and could sell to them.

We hadn't been even remotely on the Shriners' radar screen—they'd already solicited proposals, we knew, from UC San Francisco and Stanford—until Mike asked if we could also make a presentation. After all, their specialties—orthopaedics, acute burns and burn reconstruction, and spinal cord injuries (and, more recently, cleft lip surgery)—were our strengths, too. And what a collaborative opportunity it'd give us with a highly visible, extremely prominent, nationally run charitable hospital system providing free state-of-the-art medical treatment to children in Northern California, the Western United States, Northwestern Mexico and Canada. We had to try.

The Shriners essentially responded "well, sure" to Mike's query. It was a polite concession, at best.

"We didn't think there was a good possibility," Joe Tupin remembers. "We were essentially the cousins who came to dinner." But we were going to give it our best shot.

Our presentation fell to the very last, at the end of a long day for the Shriners' review team—just a few minutes and a few steps away from their anticipated day-capping libations next door.

"So we gave our presentation," Frank recalls. "They were, I think, blown away. We had letters of support, we had diagrams, we had property we could sell them, we could provide them with all kinds of back-up services and care."

They were impressed—and we were euphoric when they gave us the nod.

"I just jumped up in the air and yelled and yelled when we beat out UCSF and Stanford," Hibbard says. "That was a great triumph for UC Davis."

Frank was then charged with getting an agreement signed by the Shriners, the UC President's Office and the Davis campus.

"Believe me, it was worse than herding cats," he says. "I had to get everyone to understand it wasn't about getting something—it was about giving up things so we could get the Shriners hospital. The Office of the President was worried we were going to give [the Shriners]—true story—24 inches of right-of-way in the street we had instead of 18."

But the papers got signed, the affiliation was announced in 1990 and the Shriners flagship children's hospital opened in 1997 at 2425 Stockton Boulevard—right across the street from the UC Davis Medical Center.

Some 4,000 people attended the June 1, 1997, grand opening, including fez-wearing Shriners elatedly circling the new hospital in go-carts, Gov. Pete Wilson, Sacramento Mayor Joe Serna and former Shriners patient and "Karate Kid" film star Pat Morita. It was quite a celebration.

As I'd told the Shriners and their guests then, "We knew that we could be partners not just in medical care, but we could also share in our mutual dedication to teaching and to research."

Nearly two decades later, that partnership still thrives. *The Sacramento Bee* recently profiled Dr. David Greenhalgh, chief of burns at Shriners Hospitals for Children–Northern California ("Burn doctor helps kids heal, thrive," Aug. 28, 2014). *Bee* reporter Sammy Caiola wrote that Greenhalgh "built the facility's burn program almost singlehandedly at its start in 1997. Now, thanks to his cutting-edge medical research, it has grown into the busiest pediatric burn center on the West Coast and one of the nation's leading facilities for this specialization." And, not by accident, Dr. Greenhalgh also directs the burn division at our medical center.

This seamless collaboration—from the lab to the bedside—no doubt benefits both Shriners and UC Davis. But it's our patients who are the clear winners.

Opening in 1997 across the street from UCDMC, the Northern California Shriners Hospital for Children provides free medical care to children in Northern California, the Western United States, Northwestern Mexico and Canada. (Photo: UC Davis)

PHENOMENAL "SHOT IN THE ARM"

The second absolutely thrilling announcement—on July 31, 2007—drew a gasp and then long and loud applause from a crowd of nearly 200, including many of our nurses and med students. They'd gathered for a morning news conference in the courtyard of the medical campus's new Education Building. They'd known to expect a big announcement, but they had no idea how big.

Ed Penhoet, president of the Gordon and Betty Moore Foundation, had just revealed that the foundation was giving UC Davis $100 million to launch a new nursing school. It was our largest philanthropic grant ever and one of the largest in UC's history.

The grant's amount was clearly impressive, but its goal was even more so—to truly transform health care by producing nurses who would be leaders, educators and researchers. They would be full partners, not just delivering care but designing and implementing that care.

The new school would help to address major health care deficiencies: too few nurses (particularly as baby boomer nurses retire), too few nursing faculty (especially when teaching salaries significantly lag hospital pay), an aging (and a growing) population with greater medical needs, and a substantial number of medical-error deaths each year that nurses could help prevent.

Betty Irene Moore, for whom the new school would be named, had a very personal interest in helping to better prepare future nurses—nurses who would be interprofessional team leaders. She'd nearly died when given an insulin shot that was intended for the patient in the neighboring bed at a Bay Area hospital.

Gordon and Betty Moore Foundation President Ed Penhoet announced in 2007 that the foundation would give UC Davis $100 million to launch a new nursing school— our largest philanthropic grant ever. (Photo: Karin Higgins/UC Davis)

"They nearly had two deaths out of one medical error," said her son, Ken Moore. "That was the start of her really being interested in nursing care."

When the Moore Foundation set out to find a vision-sharing partner, we were there.

"We spent a lot of time looking at a number of other organizations who want to create nursing schools in California, and we are extremely pleased that UC Davis emerged as the best partner for us," Ed Penhoet said at the news conference.

He and Claire Pomeroy, our then-vice chancellor for human health sciences and dean of the School of Medicine, had gotten to know each other as members of the California Stem Cell Commission. They soon learned they shared a vision for nursing education,

Claire Pomeroy, vice chancellor for human health sciences and dean of the School of Medicine, and I applaud the announcement of the $100 million Moore Foundation grant for a new nursing school. (Photo: © Renée C. Byer/The Sacramento Bee/ ZUMAPRESS.com)

and their conversations (with key follow-up support from School of Medicine Executive Associate Dean Ann Bonham) ultimately led to the amazing announcement that July morning.

"This is a truly, truly wonderful gift that will change the shape and nature of health care in California for generations," said Rory Hume, then UC's provost and executive vice president of academic and health affairs. "California needs nursing leaders. It needs more nursing faculty. This is a phenomenal shot in the arm for our contributions to this great social need."

With our strong public service traditions, a nursing school was the perfect fit for us. And it resonated with me very personally. My mother, who'd only completed 8th grade before marrying my dad at 16 and starting a family two years later, decided at age 38 that she wanted to be a nurse. She went back to school and, at 42, started her nursing career—a career cut short by a heart attack just 10 years later. Through her, I knew firsthand how incredibly hardworking nurses are and how dedicated they are to their profession.

So I was especially happy to see our own nurses' reaction to the announcement that morning. They were elated—and thankful that their indispensable leadership role in medical care had been recognized with such an impressive investment.

Since that day, the school has celebrated several key milestones—the appointment of founding Dean Heather Young, the school's formal establishment in 2009, the opening of its first programs in 2010, and the graduation of its first classes (master's in 2012, doctoral in 2014).

And the Health System (and UC Davis) can mark "accomplished!" alongside yet another strategic plan goal. Long envisioned, the nursing school enables UCDHS to educate health professionals together in an interdisciplinary, collaborative way that will surely lead to higher quality of care and better patient outcomes wherever our students pursue their medical careers.

A GOAL TO GO

But one big goal remains—a School of Public Health. From natural disasters and terrorists' attacks to the rapid spread of diseases such as Ebola, tuberculosis and HIV/AIDS, the demand for public health services has surged since the days we lined up for our polio shots.

Today we need more public health professionals at all levels—locally, state-wide, nationally and globally. UC Davis can truly make a big difference here. We have exceptional expertise in just the right areas, and we have a strong tradition of collaboration across our disciplines and with our health agency partners.

I wasn't able to get our School of Public Health proposal across the finish line. But I know its time will come. The need is too great…and the UC Davis Health System's audacious story is still being written.

▶ **http://escholarship.org/uc/ucdavischancelloremeritus_books**

UC Davis Medical Center, 2014 (Photo: UC Davis)

Healing Art

A hospital visit can be a frightening experience for both patient and family. But artwork can help calm fears and create a soothing, supportive environment for medical care.

Recognizing art's special healing powers, the UC Davis Health System has commissioned artwork for its facilities' public areas since 1983—more than 2,000 pieces of original art by nearly 300 California artists.

Representative pieces in this exceptional collection are beautifully featured in the 2012 book *The Art Collection of UC Davis Health System* by Susan J. Willoughby, the collection's curator.

Here are a few of my favorites.

Jonathan Lerman's "Untitled" charcoal on Bristol board (14" x 17"), part of the UC Davis MIND Institute's special collection of artwork created by artists who themselves have neurodevelopmental disorders

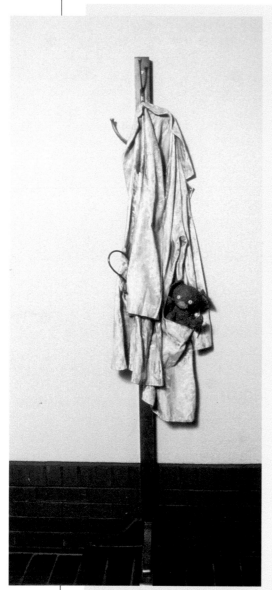

**Maru Hoeber's "Coat Tree"
bronze; 70"x21"x12"**

**Lisa Reinertson's lifesize bronze outdoor
sculpture**

Stephanie Taylor's wall-sized acrylic mural, "Untitled," provides an uplifting view for patients in the basement physical therapy gym. I know this piece well.

Yoshio Taylor's 32-foot-high tile mural, "Resurgence," greets visitors in the hospital's new main lobby.

UC DAVIS HEALTH SYSTEM LEADERS

VICE CHANCELLOR FOR HUMAN HEALTH SCIENCES AND DEAN OF THE SCHOOL OF MEDICINE

Julie A. Freischlag, 2014-present

Thomas S. Nesbitt (interim), 2013-14

Claire Pomeroy, 2004-13

DEAN OF THE SCHOOL OF MEDICINE

Joseph Silva, Jr., 1997-2004

Gerald S. Lazarus, 1993-97

James J. Castles (acting), 1992-93

Hibbard E. Williams, 1980-92

Ernest M. Gold (acting), 1980

Morton Levitt (acting), 1979

C. John Tupper (founding), 1966-79

DEAN OF THE SCHOOL OF NURSING

Heather M. Young (founding), 2009-present

MEDICAL CENTER DIRECTOR

Ann Madden Rice, 2006-present

William McGowan (acting), 2006

Robert E. Chason, 2002-06

Martha H. Marsh, 1999-2002

Robert E. Chason (interim), 1998-99

Frank J. Loge, 1984-98

Thomas B. Winston, 1978-84

Frank J. Loge (acting), 1978

Robert B. Smith, 1975-77

Baldwin G. Lamson, 1974-75 (simultaneously director of the UCLA Hospital)

Otto M. Janke, 1973-74

Iran and the Unique Potential of Academic Diplomacy

Do you think we are all terrorists?
—SOLEMNLY ASKED OF ME BY A YOUNG IRANIAN GIRL IN ISFAHAN,
   APRIL 30, 2004

SUITCASES PACKED AND TICKETS IN HAND, WE WERE TEHRAN-BOUND—DESPITE U.S. State Department cautions and the worries of our families and friends.

The worries were real. We were headed to a country deemed a member of the "Axis of Evil" by President George W. Bush. In return, Iran's Supreme Leader Ayatollah Ali Khamenei had labeled the U.S. "the most-hated Satan in the world."

As our small UC Davis delegation departed on April 25, 2004, we carried not only the concerns of those who feared for our safety but also the disapproval of others who worried about any possible political fall-out of our visiting this controversial nation.

But we weren't intending to make a political statement with this trip. And we weren't seeking publicity.

We were simply one university wanting to talk to another university about ways we could once again work together.

We'd hoped to reopen the free exchange of students and scholars, to visit our many Iranian alumni (Iran once provided the greatest share of our international students), and to increase cultural understanding.

UC Davis Delegation

- **Larry Vanderhoef, chancellor**
- **Mohammad Mohanna, Sacramento Iranian-American businessman and UC Davis Foundation trustee**
- **Neal Van Alfen, dean, College of Agricultural and Environmental Sciences**
- **Enrique Lavernia, dean, College of Engineering**
- **William Lacy, vice provost for university outreach and international programs**
- **Robert Kerr, director of international alumni and visitors**

And, in the process, we'd hoped one small step could be taken toward a return to normalcy in the Middle East.

That was my intention in 2004 when I led our small UC Davis delegation to Iran—the first such delegation, we were told, to visit Iran since that country's 1979 revolution. (Visa restrictions had prevented the president of the University of Tehran from visiting us in 2002, so we'd decided we needed to take UC Davis to Iran.)

Iranian teenagers were fun and engaging and eagerly accepted our business cards in hopes of coming to America. (Photo: Enrique Lavernia/ UC Davis)

And that was again my intention in 2008, when I returned to Iran as a member of a small Association of American Universities delegation seeking stronger academic and scientific links with Iran.

With each trip, we found the Iranian people to be warm and gracious, with lots of positive feeling for America, and our host universities to be keen on collaborating.

Our Iranian alumni, in particular, want other Iranians to see America as they saw it. They want their children to have the same opportunities they had, and are excellent ambassadors for American universities and for America, generally.

Academically, we have much to learn from one another. Many of California's 250 specialty crops, for example, originated thousands of years ago in the Fertile Crescent of Iran and other parts of the ancient Middle East. We have similar climates and similar irrigation and sustainability challenges—all ready-made areas of collaboration.

We were hopeful, when we returned in 2004, that we'd taken a fruitful first step—that we'd opened the door a bit to a country with which the U.S. had once had magnificent academic exchanges.

Not long after that visit, several Iranian scientists and university administrators traveled here to explore partnering possibilities, Nobel Peace Prize recipient and Iranian human rights activist Shirin Ebadi spoke to a Mondavi Center capacity audience about "Human Rights, Democracy and Islam," an Iranian cleric participated in a UC Davis course on Islam, Graduate School of Management Dean Nicole Biggart traveled to Iran to arrange a quarter of study here for five Sharif University students, and two Iranian children of alumni enrolled at UC Davis. Visas remained a problem, but we were beginning to make headway.

2008 RETURN TRIP

Encouraged by the bridge-building of our first visit, I returned to Iran in 2008 with a handful of other AAU university presidents. By then, Iran's political leadership had become much more conservative. This trip, there was less free-wheeling talk, more embargo-related criticisms and many more fears expressed—fears that may not have been unfounded on university campuses. Since taking office in 2005, Iranian President Mahmoud Ahmadinejad had replaced the presidents of 39 of the country's 40 top universities.

I departed Iran feeling we'd lost some ground since 2004.

Some might conclude that our efforts have been a failed experiment. Our governments remain estranged (though we each have new presidents). The United States still has no diplomatic or consular relations with Iran (ties were severed after the 1979 seizure of our embassy in Tehran). Economic sanctions remain in place over concerns with Iran's nuclear program and human rights record. The State Department continues to warn travelers about the risks of travel to Iran. And broader (and spreading) Middle East violence and political turmoil are enormously discouraging and concerning.

We briefed reporters at International House after our return from Iran. Here Dean Neal Van Alfen talks about our countries' similarities in agriculture. (Photo: Neil Michel/Axiom)

ACADEMIC DIPLOMACY

But I continue to believe in the possibilities of academic diplomacy—in its potential to build a trusting relationship between our two countries. We have so much in common. Universities across the world are dedicated to the same things—teaching and research. And their faculty belong to a scholarly community without geographic borders. That's a good place to start (and continue) a conversation.

I'm heartened to see that UC Davis' dialogue with Iranian academics persists, most recently with physics professor Warren Pickett's 2014 visit to Iran and a subsequent agreement of cooperation signed with Sharif University. Also, the number of Iranian students and scholars studying here has significantly increased, despite continuing visa difficulties and some students' concerns about returning home.

It's clear the world's universities have more work to do—more talking, more listening, more understanding. More bridge-building that I believe can make significant contributions to peace in the world.

We may be our nations' best hope.

UC Davis Students and Scholars from Iran, 1995-2014*		
Year	Students	Scholars**
1995	4	—
1996	4	—
1997	5	—
1998	3	—
1999	2	—
2000	2	—
2001	3	—
2002	5	—
2003	6	—
2004	11	5
2005	17	8
2006	23	7
2007	26	5
2008	17	21
2009	26	33
2010	34	45
2011	34	26
2012	42	24
2013	40	31
2014	48	31

Source: UC Davis Office of Services for International Students and Scholars
**Data not available for Iranian Scholars 1995-2003*

▶ http://escholarship.org/uc/ucdavischancelloremeritus_books

A Bridge-Building Champion

Moe was the catalyst.

Without Sacramento businessman and UC Davis Foundation Board trustee Moham-mad Mohanna, our 2004 trip to Iran wouldn't have been possible.

I vividly remember the November 1999 day we first met. He'd hosted an event to raise scholarship funds for Iranian-American students—a gathering that included tra-ditional dance, dress and songs of Persia, all performed by UC Davis students. At the event's end, several of those students came to me with a friendly petition. Their parents had come to America during Iran's 1979 revolution and, once in the U.S., were careful not to teach their children Farsi (the language of Iran) or to share much about that country's culture. They'd wanted their children to become Americanized as quickly as possible. But now these students were young adults and yearned to better understand their cultural history and to learn Farsi. (The campus figured out a way, collaborating with Sacramento City College, to offer that language/culture course—and many other similar courses for first-generation Americans of other cultures.)

Moe understood the Iranian-American students' burgeon-ing interest in their shared culture.

Born in Iran, he came to the U.S. when he was about their age, determined to become another "only in America" suc-cess story. Cut off from his family financially, he emigrated to a poor Boston neighborhood where he lived and worked

> "History will show that UC Davis was at the forefront, that it was the champion of dialogue."
>
> —Mohammad Mohanna, Sacramento businessman and UC Davis Founda-tion Board trustee

as a janitor in a Volunteers of America halfway house. He learned English, finished school and saved enough money to buy his first piece of real estate—a fixer-upper apartment building—by the time he was 22. That was the beginning of his long and successful career as a Sacramento developer and as an advocate for the poor and the homeless.

And that 1999 Iranian scholarship fundraiser was the beginning of our long-lasting friendship—and the launching of our many, many conversations about Iran. In the 1970s, I'd been the graduate adviser for several Iranian students at the University of Il-linois and knew how exceptionally well-prepared they were for their studies. But Iran's 1979 revolution and takeover of our embassy had put an abrupt end to our academic exchanges.

For more than two decades, I'd waited patiently for the immigration gates to open once again. But faculty and student exchange opportunities between the U.S. and Iran seemed impossibly stalled.

So Moe and I teamed up. We both believed it was time—and essential—to begin a dialogue once again with Iran's best universities.

Moe carried a message from me to the president of the University of Tehran, inviting him to visit UC Davis. President Khalili Araghi had hoped to be on his way here in 2002 but then heightened post-9/11 fears prevented him from obtaining a visa.

So I said, not a little naively, "Since he can't come here, why don't we go there?"

For starters, with no embassy and no formal U.S. relations with Iran, we had our own visa issues. But Pakistani alum Rashid Ahmad helped us obtain the necessary documents in near-miracle time. And Moe enlisted Professor Ahmad Iravani, professor of Islamic law at The Catholic University of America, to help frame the trip and set up appointments at four leading universities in Iran. To my amazement—still—it all fell into place.

The intentions of our small delegation were simple. We just wanted to "break bread," as Moe expressed it, and to start a conversation that we hoped could one day lead to renewed academic alliances.

Without Mohammad Mohanna, our bridge-building trip to Iran wouldn't have been possible. (Photo: Karin Higgins/UC Davis)

Everywhere we went, every new group with whom we interacted, Moe, in Farsi, introduced us and our intentions in Iran. He surely must have done this well because we were always warmly welcomed.

A few months after our return, Moe spoke about our trip at the Fall 2004 Convocation:

"Ladies and gentlemen, I am really proud to say as an American I carried your message, the message of democracy, equality, human rights and dignity, to Iran. They were very pleased to hear one of their sons is bringing that message. They are thirsty for knowledge; they are eager to have a dialogue; they are tired of competition.

"In this country I have been taught how to compete, and I am a fierce competitor. It is my hope that we learn to cooperate, to have compassion. When competition yields to compassion and cooperation, we may achieve some greatness.... I'm asking all of the foreign students here today: you are an ambassador of the United States to your nations. Take the message of democracy, tolerance and human rights to your countries and let us build a better nation."

Today, Moe says UC Davis continues to be regarded in Iran as "an institution that did what was right in education—not politics, not religion. History will show that UC Davis was at the forefront, that it was the champion of dialogue."

Moe and I still talk about our hopes for Iran, and, fancifully, I dream about another trip.

Moe says he'd like me to be there when the ribbon is cut on a reopened U.S. embassy in Tehran.

I'd be there. In a heartbeat.

Into Iran:
Excerpts from My 2004 Iran Journal

APRIL 25, 2004: WE'RE ON OUR WAY

Well, we're off, setting out for the San Francisco Airport on the first leg of our 24-hour journey to Tehran. We carry the concerns of our families and colleagues who fear for our safety and the disapproval of some who worry about any possible political fall-out of visiting what has been deemed by President Bush an "Axis of Evil" country.

The Iranian population is remarkably young—half under the age of 20 and 70 percent under 30. Boys and girls, and men and women, gather separately in public. (Photo: Larry Vanderhoef/UC Davis)

We've talked at length among ourselves and with others about the wisdom of our trip, about whether our goals outweigh any risk we may be assuming in traveling to the Middle East right now. We remain convinced we should go, that our desire to reestablish academic ties, to reopen the free exchange of students and scholars and to further cultural understanding overrides our concerns. Our conversations with our Iranian hosts and with the U.S. state department provide us with sufficient reassurance of a safe trip.

Our journey actually began nearly five years ago, when fellow traveler Moe Mohanna (a Sacramento businessman and current member of the UC Davis Foundation Board) hosted an event to raise scholarship funds for Iranian-American students. That gathering eventually led to an invitation to the president of the University of Tehran to visit UC Davis; but when he attempted that trip in 2002, he was denied a visa. So we decided then that we would take UC Davis to Iran.

So here we are, all six of us (Moe Mohanna; Neal Van Alfen, dean of the College of Agricultural and Environmental Sciences; Enrique Lavernia, dean of the College of Engineering; Bill Lacy, vice provost for university outreach and international programs; Bob Kerr, director of international alumni and visitors; and me), unsure what we'll experience this next week but eager to begin a dialogue. We're not going to Iran to make a political statement, nor are we seeking publicity. We're simply one university wanting to talk to another university about ways in which we can work together. And, perhaps in the process, one small step can be taken toward a return to normalcy in the Middle East.

... Once we arrive at the Lufthansa departure gate area, our concern about journeying to Iran dissipates. In fact, our fears seem to be left behind in the U.S.

Enrique wonders if the only time there might be a problem with trips to the Middle East is if one asks about the laws and rules, as we did. Neal mentions that some of our faculty are planning to attend an international conference in Iran next year—organized from another country, with individuals coming from all over the world.

Neal also mentions that our California crops are much the same as Iran's, and that many of our 250 specialty crops originated in Iran and other parts of the Mid-

Intricate brass metalwork and finely woven Persian rugs still beckon in Silk Road bazaars dating back to the days of Marco Polo. California's crops are much the same as Iran's, featured here in a Tehran food shop. Many of the state's 250 specialty crops originated in Iran and other parts of the Middle East thousands of years ago. (Photos: Larry Vanderhoef/UC Davis)

dle East thousands of years ago. Pistachios, for example, came to California some 80 years ago by way of Iran. With similar climates and irrigation and sustainability challenges, we've much to learn from each other.

As we taxi down the runway, the plane suddenly screeches to a halt. We hear another plane land or take off nearby. Our plane resumes its taxiing, but more slowly this time. I immediately think of some of the troubling e-mails we'd received since pre-trip stories appeared in our local newspapers. But then off we fly. ...

APRIL 26: MIDWAY THERE

We land in Frankfurt without incident and make our way to the hotel for about four hours sleep before returning to the airport for the next leg of the trip to Tehran. I end up sitting next to an Iranian-American woman who's from Davis, used to work for UC Davis and has a daughter working at UC Irvine—the proverbial small world. She's returning to Iran for the one-year anniversary of her mother's death. ...

APRIL 27: AT LAST, WE ARRIVE

We touch down in Tehran and are greeted at the end of the jetway by the director general of the University of Tehran's Office of International Relations and by the university's chief of protocol, who is also with the Ministry of Science, Research and Technology. While we wait for our luggage, we chat a bit with our two hosts. Mohammad wears a black shirt under his suit coat—a sign his father has recently

In Tehran, I chatted with a police officer who made quick friends with our UC Davis travelers. (Photo: Enrique Lavernia)

died. He will wear this shirt for 40 days without shaving. Both when his father died, and at the 40-day mourning mark, he will host a lunch for friends of his father. He served 900 lunches that first day and expects to do the same 40 days hence. And, on the one-year anniversary, there'll be another recognition of his father's death.

We see occasional armed soldiers, but certainly no more than we have seen in other countries—especially, for example, Taiwan but also South Korea.

We arrive at our hotel at 4 a.m. but find our rooms aren't ready. After phone calls home, we're soon to bed, anticipating our visits later today with the president of the University of Tehran and its engineering faculty.

After four hours sleep and a breakfast buffet featuring sausage and olives, we head to the Central Library and Document Center at the University of Tehran. We primarily spend our time in the section of the library

The shah's summer palace grounds and former polo field—once reserved for Iran's elite—are now enjoyed by everyday Iranians. (Photos: Larry Vanderhoef/UC Davis)

dedicated to saving old books for future readers ("old" here means up to 1,400 years old).

We then meet the president of the university, Faraji-Dana, for lunch. He's a very impressive 45-year-old, much interested in any relationships we might build. He notes his university is pursuing a "2 and 2" exchange program with Indiana University/Purdue University in Indianapolis and also a one-person plant taxonomy exchange with UC Berkeley. We have to find out more about both.

The afternoon is devoted to meetings with the engineering faculty. It's very clear

Workers were seen mowing the palace's expansive grounds by hand mowers or scythes—part of a government effort to provide jobs, officials said. (Photo: Larry Vanderhoef/UC Davis)

the trade embargo has made it difficult for them to buy new equipment or to obtain replacement parts. Effects show up on the streets, too, where cars are mostly pre-1979. Occasionally, though, their laboratory equipment is state-of-the-art, likely purchased through other countries.

President Faraji and I talk again that evening. He's very much wanting to establish collaborative ties and hopes those ties will expand to other universities.

The relationship between our two countries is certainly complicated and challenging, from the 1979 revolution and overthrow of the shah, the hostage-taking at our embassy and our support of Iraq and Saddam Hussein during the eight-year Iran-Iraq War—a war that stopped, as Moe Mohanna says, because the people of both countries just got tired of war.

We talk as well about how Iran's left-leaning potential candidates for parliament have been eased out of the opportunity to run by the Supreme Council—the country's 12 highest-ranking ayatollahs, who are responsible for keeping the government's actions within the constraints of Islam. So the government will ease back toward the right after the next election and the country's president will finish his second term and be unable to run again. It's interesting that the people here are not expecting any of these changes to be huge or unusual, but simply the result of a government that will shift, as all governments do, but in this case toward the right by selection and support of right-leaning candidates.

We end the day at a dinner gathering of some 80 people with connections to UC Davis, including the deputy minister of agriculture, who is an alum. The dinner features traditional chicken/lamb kabobs and a superb mushroom soup that I could make a whole meal of. We exchange gifts and listen to traditional Iranian music drawn from ancient mystic writings—it's beautiful, quite unique to the Middle East. ...

APRIL 28: OFF TO MORE VISITS

We're off to visit the University of Tehran's agriculture faculty this morning. The dean (a very funny, interesting guy) wants us to visit every department, but that just isn't possible—though we manage to cover a lot of ground before lunch.

We split up in the afternoon, with Neal, Bill and Bob staying to talk further with the ag faculty, while Moe, Enrique and I visit a brand-new hospital built by the Rahimian family, which has roots in Iran, associations in Sacramento and has sent two sons to UC Davis. The hospital was built in an area of relatively poor people without easy access to medical care. A while back, the Rahimian family also built a high school for girls, with about 1,000 now enrolled.

On the way to the hospital, it feels as if one of the wheels of our car suddenly goes badly, badly out of balance. As luck would have it, a tow truck just happens by and we are quickly fetched by Laudan Rahimian, sister of Majid Rahimian Before we leave, we take an outdoor picture with most of the nurses on duty. For the second time, I make the cultural mistake of attempting to shake the hand of one of them to whom we have given a UC Davis pen. When I first met Laudan, she put her hand out to make it clear that, in her case, she would recognize our custom.

Laudan's husband drives us back to our hotel at breakneck speeds—up to 165 kilometers an hour (I haven't done the conversion, but it's close to 100 miles per hour) on a freeway where most people are going 65 miles per hour. The lane markers are not much more than suggestions, with often four lanes of traffic squeezed into three. It's just the normal way of things, but if you're not used to it, it's very worrisome. More than a couple of times, Enrique and I simultaneously yell something like "watch out" (or an internationally understood equivalent).

At 8:30 p.m. we depart for the parliament and dinner with the brother of President Khatami. Our conversation has many pregnant pauses; the three individuals with

Khatami don't speak at all. But after dinner, we go outside to have tea. Khatami and I talk lots about his predictions for the future of universities, why he thinks Iran is viewed so negatively by the U.S., why any kind of "revolution" by students now would be completely different from the one in 1979 (they're more educated now, he says, and have a better realization of what can and can't be accomplished by the overthrow of any government). He recognizes that, in this stage of Iran's evolution, theocracy is most likely to work but that it might not be the form of government that would necessarily serve well in the future. He feels very strongly there are not many ways to break down the stereotype that people in the world have of Iran, but believes the "university track" is a way that could be successful. ...

APRIL 29: ON TO THE 'CAL TECH OF IRAN'

After a breakfast of hard-boiled eggs, cold meats, cheeses, coffee, juices, milk and cold cereals, we set out for Sharif University of Technology—the Cal Tech of Iran. While women are as prevalent in Iranian universities as men (in fact, women slightly outnumber men), only about 30 percent of the students at technology universities are female (just as in the U.S.).

The university's president expresses frustration that Iran has been singled out as part of the "Axis of Evil." He points to the culture, traditions and history of Persia (primarily Iran, he says, but also Armenia and Turkey) as different from Arab countries. Those countries do not share the ancient history and culture of Iran, the birthplace of most history and culture in the world, he says. Neither do Iranians support Al-Queda or the Taliban, he says, noting mostly it's peace that's desired and a fair understanding of each other.

After lunch, we depart for Isfahan and visits to two other universities. From the air, we see essentially a salt plain; as we near the city, we see irrigated crops and mud adobe-type construction. The towns outside Isfahan look very poor; the city itself seems an oasis of trees, grass and flowers. The hotel is very nice (much nicer than the buildings around it), with televisions with perhaps 12 channels—most in Farsi, with soccer matches, an occasional NBA basketball game, "tame" American movies, one or two German-language channels, and BBC and CNN. We see pictures of the bombing of Fallujah on Iranian channels and on BBC and CNN. The U.S. is not getting a good review.

Dinner is with several alumni—including one who has an interest in the travel industry and has moved to Iran to be ready when it once again becomes an important destination. Another has gone into the business of university-related research parks here.

Our evening ends with a stroll at the ancient "lighted bridges" (one is 280 years old, another 480 years old). Groups of young people stop and sing under their arches, to the applause of others nearby. ...

APRIL 30: A MARATHON DAY

Today will be a very, very long day. We will not go to bed again until we are home. Ahead are visits to the University of Isfahan (its president is a UC Riverside grad) and Isfahan University of Technology (its president is a UC Berkeley grad), as well as some sightseeing, and then a flight back to Tehran for an alumni/going-away gathering.

As we walk the city streets, unaccompanied by our hosts, we are treated warmly and graciously by adults and with curiosity and respect by children. We are struck with how young the population is—50 percent under the age of 20 and 70 percent under 30. The teenagers are fun and engaging but sometimes very solemnly forthright. I will never forget, to the day I die, a young girl asking me, "Do you think we are all terrorists?" Other young people ask how they can come to America and eagerly accept our business cards.

We visit mosques, bazaars, palaces and a Christian church and enjoy our conversations. We see that men and women rarely mix, at least publicly— and that women are covered except for their faces, with some younger women wearing blue jeans as slacks and also makeup.

At an alumni gathering that evening at the Rahimians' home, we meet with about 40 people with UC ties. All of the alums we've met this trip are proud of their alma maters and treasure their

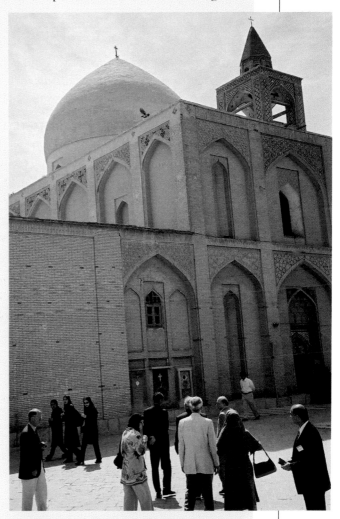

An Armenian Christian church augments Isfahan's many Islamic mosques as a place of worship. (Photo: Larry Vanderhoef/UC Davis)

memories of their time in the U.S. They want their children to have the same opportunities they had, and are excellent ambassadors for American universities and for America, generally. They want, as well, for other Iranians to see America as they saw it and not as we've also been negatively represented in the media around the world.

We depart the party well after midnight and head to the airport for a 3:05 a.m. flight. ...

MAY 1: HEADING HOME/NEXT STEPS

We use our Frankfurt layover time to try to assess what we've experienced and to see possible next steps in forging a relationship with the Iranian universities we've visited.

We're all struck with the high quality of the faculty and students—their admissions standards, in fact, are tougher than UC's. Graduate study there is all done in English, and passing an English exam is part of the admissions process.

While this trip is a fruitful first step, we recognize the considerable challenges that lie ahead. Perhaps the biggest is the current severe visa restrictions that make it virtually impossible for Iranians to travel to this country.

But one potential exchange possibility is the "2 and 2" program, where Iranian students would spend the first two years at their home university taking courses approved by UC and then come to America, to UC Davis, for the remaining two years of their program—giving us a bit more time to resolve the visa problem.

Another possibility is sending our students there, perhaps for summer study.

A third possibility would involve exchange of scholars based on real needs they have and we have—truly a two-way street. And perhaps, as well, we can establish a formal alumni chapter in Iran to help us recruit outstanding students, host visiting students and scholars and provide internship opportunities.

After nearly 22 hours in the air and another two hours on I-80, we arrive home tired but energized. In this initial visit, we didn't sign agreements or contracts with our Iranian colleagues, but we sat together, we ate together, we discussed our separate countries and cultures together, and we came to better understand our universities, our similarities and differences, and our shared interest in a community of scholars without borders. I hope our trip moves us a step closer together and, in the words of Sen. J. William Fulbright, in some small way helps "turn nations into people."

A Principled Community

There was so much distrust. Getting things committed to paper was crucial.
—FORMER STUDENT AFFAIRS VICE CHANCELLOR THOMAS DUTTON
ABOUT HOW UC DAVIS' PRINCIPLES OF COMMUNITY CAME TO BE

TENSIONS MOUNTED. TEMPERS FLARED. DISTRUST INTENSIFIED AS CULTURAL beliefs collided.

It was the late 1980s, and the university's stepped-up efforts to recruit a more diverse class of students were beginning to yield results.

We were evolving then as a campus community, and sometimes painfully so, as people of different races, cultures, religions, genders, sexual orientation, socio-economic back-grounds and political points of view increasingly interacted. That interaction was just what the campus needed, but it wasn't easy.

That decade, the number of African American, Chicano, Latino and Native American undergrads grew from 876 to 2,351, from 9.7 percent to 12.7 percent of all undergraduates—not nearly what it should have been to mirror the state's demographics (and far less than what it is today), but enough then to establish a visible toehold and to provide a plat-form for vociferously advocating greater progress.

Vice Chancellor Tom Dutton responds to students gathered March 7, 1990, to protest the removal of a symbolic shanty from the Memorial Union Patio. (Photo: Tom McNeill/The California Aggie)

Tom Dutton, our vice chancellor for student affairs then, recalls many a strained meet-ing—and one in particular where a student "went on and on about all the bad things the campus was doing and what we weren't doing that we should be doing. I just said, 'That's not true.' We really got into it because I challenged her integrity and she was challenging mine. I think over time what helped us to break through that was the recognition of the importance of communication, of talking with each other."

But Tom knew communication wasn't enough. Administrators and students came and went, and so too the trust they had built.

It was also essential, he believed, to put into writing the university's lasting commitment to be a community that valued diversity, that rejected discrimination, and that affirmed freedom of expression but within the bounds of civility and respect.

It was Tom, early on, who sowed the seeds of our campus-wide Principles of Community.

NO UNIVERSITY-WIDE MODELS

When our drafting work began in the spring of 1988, there were no university-wide models—only statements developed by student affairs offices for use primarily in the residence halls, where conflicts were most likely to surface first. Our own student housing office had created such a statement, which the Executive Council of the Associated Students of UC Davis modified and adopted in June 1988.

With a proposed draft in hand to start a campus-wide conversation, former Assistant Vice Chancellor for Student Affairs Yvonne Marsh in May 1988 wrote to the chairs of campus organizations concerned about diversity to ask for their help in developing and adopting a UC Davis statement of Principles of Community.

"As the campus becomes a much more diverse community…the potential for divisive conflict is a concern," she wrote. "There are many ways the campus is preparing for and

Assistant Vice Chancellor Yvonne Marsh (pictured with her mother, Mabel Brooks, and daughter, Tamara Marsh) as she received the campus's first Black History Month Tribute in February 1997. (Photo: Todd Hammond/The Davis Enterprise)

encouraging diversity…. A statement of Principles of Community which we actively promote in our programs and activities might be an additional affirmative step toward a truly pluralistic community."

Yvonne got the early response she needed and then set off to involve more faculty, staff and student leaders in drafting just the right words—without running afoul of the First Amendment's guarantee of free speech—to affirm the kind of community we wanted.

Then-UC President David Gardner felt such statements—which were beginning to pick up steam in the UC system—wouldn't withstand a constitutional challenge. But we knew our legal limitations, and recognized we couldn't put forth these principles as rules or regulations. They were principles—guidelines developed by and for our community to help us

Vice Chancellor Tom Dutton addresses a crowd of nearly 400 at a March 7, 1990, protest. (Photo: Tom McNeill/The California Aggie)

create the environment we believed essential to our success. Nonetheless, we were careful to run our words by the university's attorneys.

The back-and-forth of drafts—remember, this was the before-e-mail era—took some time as groups met, marked up text, and, by snail-mail, sent revisions back for other groups' consideration.

Yvonne persevered, referencing the statement's "incredible evolution" in a Nov. 2, 1989, memo to which she attached "a completely new draft…[that] emphasizes mutual respect and cooperation rather than prohibition and sanction." She needed a quick turnaround because a campus-city subcommittee was about to consider developing a similar statement after the City of Davis Human Relations Commission issued a report of racial incidents within the city.

Such reports weren't isolated to Davis and its campus. A national study of campus life that year by the Carnegie Foundation for the Advancement of Teaching and the American Council on Education found a "growing inclination among some students to use words, not as the key to understanding, but as weapons of assault," said Carnegie Foundation President Ernest Boyer in a Jan. 18, 1990, speech. "And this breakdown of civility is revealing itself most frequently in racial, ethnic and sexual slurs."

Boyer's report, formally issued in May 1990, called on campuses to develop "a set of agreed-upon standards to guide the conduct of all members of the community and give direction to the institution overall."

We were already there. On April 20, 1990, Chancellor Ted Hullar gathered the leaders of our faculty, staff and student groups in his office for an official signing of the UC Davis Principles of Community.

Yvonne today particularly acknowledges the advocacy of former Academic Senate Chair Charlie Nash and the wordsmithery of his office's Bea Crockett for getting the document over the finish line—and the Student Affairs organizational structure Tom put into place that "brought us together at critical places so we all became part of a group trying to create the kind of community that was reflected in the Principles."

No doubt Charlie, Bea and Tom played key roles. But Yvonne was our true-north navigator. She kept us on course and ultimately delivered a document that has served us well for more than two decades.

CLASS BOYCOTT AND HUNGER STRIKE

Just weeks after their signing, the Principles of Community were tested. On May 1, 1990, some 200 students boycotted classes, calling for greater campus diversity. On May 14, four of our students—José Quinones, Andrea Gaytan, Gopal Dayeneni and Ahmanal Dorsey—launched a hunger strike on the north apron of Mrak Hall. It ended six days later with an agreement to establish a Cross Cultural Center, to guarantee in writing the addition of six full-time faculty positions in each of the campus's four ethnic studies programs (a commitment made by Chancellor Hullar in January 1989), and to formally examine concerns about racism in the Spanish department and elsewhere on campus.

Associate Vice Chancellor Griselda Castro in the new Student Community Center's welcoming lobby. (Photo: Gregory Urquiaga/ UC Davis)

These strike-ending promises were kept, though progress generally was made in increments—a particularly frustrating timeframe for students counting down the time to their departure. In fact, just one of the four hunger strikers hadn't yet graduated by the time the promised Cross Cultural Center opened in fall 1992 in the renovated former Agricultural Extension Building.

To students, the university's pace too often seemed glacial—and deliberately so.

But they had a strong advocate

Students (seated from left) Andrea Gaytan, Ahmanal Dorsey, Gopal Daycnenl and José Quinones conducted a six-day hunger strike on the north apron of Mrak Hall in May 1990. (Photo: Neil Michel/Axlom)

in Griselda Castro, then an Educational Opportunity Program adviser in the College of Letters and Science and chair of the Chicano Studies advisory committee—and a steady, interceding presence at strike teach-ins and candlelight vigils on the Mrak lawn. She helped rescue hunger-striking students from potential academic trouble after their strike-interrupted quarter. And she helped avert a second hunger strike more than a decade later by students impatient for a permanent home for the Cross Cultural Center.

In March 2002, Griselda asked ASUCD President Chia-Saun Lai to consider including the center in the Campus Expansion Initiative, which had been fast-tracked to seek students' financial support of a move to Division I athletics. Chia-Saun embraced the idea—and ultimately so did students. The initiative passed, helping to make possible the construction of a Student Community Center, a permanent facility to foster student diversity and inclusion—and to truly symbolize our Principles of Community.

A SPECIAL SPACE FOR BUILDING COMMUNITY

Opened in January 2012, the Student Community Center is home to the Cross Cultural Center; the Lesbian, Gay, Bisexual, Transgender Resource Center; the Student Recruitment and Retention Center; the Women's Resources and Research Center outreach office; the Undergraduate Research Center; the Community Outreach satellite office; and the UC Davis McNair Scholars Program office—all previously located in inadequate or out-of-the-way spaces. A media lab, computer classrooms, multi-purpose room, meet-

Opened in January 2012, the Student Community Center stands as a concrete expression of our Principles of Community. (Photo: Gregory Urquiaga/UC Davis)

ing space, reading and study lounge, outdoor balconies, reflection space and garden, and student-run café also draw students to this heart-of-the-campus building that's kitty-corner to the Silo, across from the Chemistry Building and just a half-block from a Unitrans bus hub. Its expansive, welcoming lobby intentionally emulates Griselda's grandmother's courtyard in Mexico—a central, communal space that drew everyone together from different parts of the house.

So why did it take 22 years to turn the vision for such a transformative facility—a concrete expression of our Principles of Community—into reality?

Griselda, speaking at the center's May 18, 2012, dedication, posited that "effecting permanent and long-lasting change in a major research university is not a 50-yard dash; it's a marathon. It takes student and campus leaders who are willing to safeguard institutional memory and pass the torch to others."

As well, in those 22 years the campus's diversity continued to grow and evolve. With Griselda's shepherding, we ultimately were able to create something even better than we could have imagined in 1990.

And she's pleased—very pleased. Debunking the "ethnic ghetto" or "diversity dump" concerns that she confronted early on, the center broadly draws students from all corners of the campus.

"I was determined to build in things that were for all students so that the Student Community Center would be a natural part of the campus's fabric," Griselda, now retired, says. "When students come to the center, you can see the energy. They're working together, building community, building relationships, building connections. That's the beauty of it. It's what makes it a community center as opposed to a place where you go to get a cup of coffee."

The new building has got to be uniquely satisfying for one of its residents—1990 hunger-striker Andrea Gaytan, appointed assistant director of the Cross Cultural Center in 2009. She graduated before the doors to the hunger-strike-promised Cross Cultural Center opened. Now the CCC is prominently located in the new Student Community Center, with several other community-building centers as neighbors (including the AB540 and Undocumented Student Center, which Andrea currently heads).

"It's fulfilling to see that what student activists did had a larger impact, had a lasting legacy," Andrea says. "I'm so excited to see a building like this. We all have equitable spaces and work together collaboratively—and nobody else had to have a hunger strike to have their spaces established."

ASPIRATIONS, NOT RULES

The Principles of Community truly speak to the special spirit and culture of the campus.

"They create a sense of community that you can't legislate," says Rahim Reed, associate executive vice chancellor for campus community relations. "Because they're aspirational, because people aspire to something higher, that's what makes them unique, that's what makes their value immeasurable."

Associate Executive Vice Chancellor Rahim Reed discusses the Campus Community Book Project with Mikael Villalobos, the project's director. (Photo: Gregory Urquiaga/UC Davis)

Rahim came to UC Davis in 2001 from the University of Florida, particularly drawn by the campus's approach to creating community and intent on making the Principles "something you lived and breathed every day."

An early and lasting idea was the Campus Community Book Project. Shortly after the Sept. 11, 2001, terrorist attacks, we borrowed Purdue University's "common reading program" for its newest students but expanded it to the Nth degree—engaging not just the freshman class but the entire campus and surrounding community in reading and discussing a single book. Especially that first year, when our nation was so fractured and frightened, it was important to find ways for people who were different to be able to talk to one another without feeling threatened or intimidated.

The book project took off, aided by the strong foundation provided by the Principles of Community, Rahim says. "The Principles and the book project intertwined, and they both helped each other grow."

> **"We recognize that each of us has an obligation to the community of which we have chosen to be a part."**
> **—Principles of Community excerpt**

The Principles periodically are publicly reaffirmed and signed by current administrative, student, faculty and staff leaders; celebrated each year during a special week; discussed with new students and their parents at orientation; and are brought to life in an interactive on-line course for staff and faculty.

More than two decades after their adoption, the Principles of Community remain important guideposts, heralded when we are at our best and invoked when we fall short.

While there's no formal sanction for their violation, they do give us a powerful personal platform.

"The Principles tell us that an affront to one member of the campus community is an affront to us all," Rahim says. "They empower us to step up or speak out or do something to show our support for the person who's been mistreated and to show our opposition to the conduct that's violating our Principles."

We—*we*—have the power.

And we've made a principled promise to one another.

Student Kayla Green sings at a 2013 "Know Your Song" Principles of Community Week event that included discussion of the historical significance of James Weldon Johnson's song "Lift Every Voice and Sing." (Photo: Joe Proudman/UC Davis)

UNIVERSITY OF CALIFORNIA, DAVIS

PRINCIPLES OF COMMUNITY

APRIL 20, 1990

The University of California, Davis, is first and foremost an institution of learning and teaching, committed to serving the needs of society. Our campus community reflects and is a part of a society comprising all races, creeds and social circumstances. The successful conduct of the university's affairs requires that every member of the university community acknowledge and practice the following basic principles:

We affirm the dignity inherent in all of us, and we strive to maintain a climate of justice marked by respect for each other. We acknowledge that our society carries within it historical and deep-rooted misunderstandings and biases, and therefore we will endeavor to foster mutual understanding among the many parts of our whole.

We affirm the right of freedom of expression within our community and also affirm our commitment to the highest standards of civility and decency towards all. We recognize the right of every individual to think and speak as dictated by personal belief, to express any idea, and to disagree with or counter another's point of view, limited only by university regulations governing time, place and manner. We promote open expression of our individuality and our diversity within the bounds of courtesy, sensitivity and respect.

We confront and reject all manifestations of discrimination, including those based on race, ethnicity, gender, age, disability, sexual orientation, religious or political beliefs, status within or outside the university, or any of the other differences among people which have been excuses for misunderstanding, dissension or hatred. We recognize and cherish the richness contributed to our lives by our diversity. We take pride in our various achievements, and we celebrate our differences.

We recognize that each of us has an obligation to the community of which we have chosen to be a part. We will strive to build a true community of spirit and purpose based on mutual respect and caring.

THEODORE L. HULLAR
Chancellor

STEVEN JOHNS
President, ASUCD

CHARLES NASH
Chair, Academic Senate

PIERRE DU VAIR
Chair, Graduate Student Association

DAVID HELLER
Chair, Staff Assembly

JANE KIMBALL
Chair, Academic Staff Organization

MARGARET HAYES
Chair, UCDMC Staff Assembly

Facing—and Living in the Shadow of—No-Confidence Votes

This vote is no more than a symbolic gesture of frustration aimed at the wrong target.
—PHILIP KASS, PROFESSOR OF VETERINARY MEDICINE,
    AT FEB. 21, 2006, SENATE TOWN HALL MEETING

This is a marvelous opportunity for people who want to get a couple of licks in and who've been waiting for years and years to do it.
—JOHN VOHS, SENIOR LECTURER AND FORMER ACADEMIC SENATE
    CHAIR, AT FEB. 21, 2006, SENATE TOWN HALL MEETING

I KNEW IT WAS COMING. I'D READ THE NEWSPAPER REPORTS OF THE signature-gathering effort.

But, even so, I wasn't prepared when, like more than 2,500 other Academic Senate members, I opened that Feb. 1, 2006, 9:08 a.m. email from Senate Secretary Susan Kauzlarich.

"You are hereby notified that the Secretary has received a written request for a mail ballot signed by more than 50 members of the Davis Division of the Academic Senate asking that the following 'Resolution for a Vote of No Confidence against Larry N. Vanderhoef, Chancellor, UC Davis' be voted on by the entire Davis Division of the Senate."

An overflow crowd of more than 125 attended my Jan. 27, 2006, Brown Bag Chat to hear me address the executive compensation controversy. (Photo: Karin Higgins/UC Davis)

The "whereas" clauses, condemning my settlement of a potential discrimination lawsuit threatened by a departing vice chancellor, accused me of unethical behavior that had caused irreparable damage to the image of UC Davis.

"Condemn." "No confidence." The words took my breath away.

I understood the concerns underlying the resolution—concerns that were exacerbated by previously undisclosed UC-wide executive compensation practices reported in December 2005 by the *San Francisco Chronicle*, including my separation agreement the prior June with a vice chancellor I'd hired seven years earlier. That agreement, settling claims of racial and gender discrimination and approved by UC's Office of the General Counsel, subsequently was widely criticized as inappropriately generous and helped trigger a regental audit, legislative hearings and newspaper editorials on UC's executive compensation excesses.

I was heartsick at the agreement's hurtful impact on our campus. As I'd told our faculty at the Feb. 3, 2006, Academic Senate meeting, my intentions had been only to protect the university. I'd wanted to avoid the financial and political costs of extended litigation; I'd wanted to avert the damaging impact of discrimination allegations, no matter their merit, on the recruitment and retention of our faculty, staff and students; and I'd wanted to prevent the university from losing ground in its preparations for our first comprehensive fundraising campaign, a critically important undertaking for our campus.

"I can appreciate how all of us now, with the gift of hindsight, might have chosen a different course," I'd said at the meeting. "But at the time, with the best information available, I had to make decisions. Would I make those same decisions over again, knowing what I know now? No, I would not. And, in addition, I very much regret the turmoil this agreement has caused, and its hurtful impact on you and on our university. For that, I am very sorry."

My apology was from the heart. I love this campus and would never intentionally harm it. I hoped the faculty could see that and could forgive.

The next six weeks—just the blink of an eye, you might think—were interminably agonizing as I awaited the posting of "pro" and "con" statements, a Senate town hall meeting, the mailing and return of ballots, the vote tally and, finally, the announced outcome. Though the ballot referenced just one issue—the separation agreement—I knew that surely there'd been something that'd occurred on my 12-year watch that hadn't been to someone's liking. Put together enough of those individual irritations and you could quickly get to a majority vote of no confidence, I feared.

I'll be forever grateful to the many campus family members who sent supportive messages over those six weeks—messages that came to me at exactly the right time, almost like they'd dropped from heaven.

Likewise, I remain indebted to the many faculty who contributed "con" statements to the Senate's web site, opposing the no-confidence resolution. Chief among them was Dan Simmons, professor of law and then-chair of the Davis Division of the Academic Senate, who wrote: "My several conversations with Chancellor Vanderhoef regarding [this] matter convince me that he acted forthrightly in what he believed was the best interest of the Campus and the University."

Their influence was surely felt in the Senate's March 13 announcement that the no-confidence motion had been rejected, 70 percent to 30 percent. Favored by 320 voters and opposed by 734, the advisory measure drew 1,054 valid ballots from 2,513 eligible Academic Senate members (faculty holding tenured, tenure-track and emeriti positions).

I was heartened, relieved and appreciative. But I understood the concerns that prompted the vote and committed to working with the regents, the president and other chancellors to make the executive compensation changes that were (and, I believe, continue to be) needed to ensure the university's accountability.

SHADOW CONSEQUENCES

Like me, presidents and chancellors most often survive no-confidence votes. But that's not to say those votes don't have consequences.

Only a masochist would want to invite another such humiliating public rebuke.

And there lies the danger—the temptation to duck future decisions that might be unpopular. With wounds still fresh, who wouldn't want to avoid further controversy?

But it's essential that university leaders continue to put their campuses' well-being above

The Jan. 27, 2006, Brown Bag Chat also drew local news media, including KOVR Channel 13 reporter Stephanie Nishikawa (far left against the wall). (Photo: Karin Higgins/UC Davis)

Communications Senior Lecturer Emeritus John Vohs (middle) speaks about the no-confidence resolution at the Feb. 21, 2006, Senate Town Hall attended by about 45 faculty members. (Photo: Karin Higgins/UC Davis)

their own and not shy away from difficult decisions that must be made. I was lucky to have one particularly savvy mentor on this matter—James H. Meyer, who served as UC Davis chancellor from 1969 to 1987. Over and over I had heard from Jim, "This is what I'd like to do, but this is what I have to do." The university always came first—not future career goals or personal popularity—when making university decisions.

I knew I could not let my no-confidence vote experience affect—in even the tiniest, most insignificant way—the decisions I had to make for the university.

So I took an especially deep breath during the 2008 provost search when it became apparent to me that none of our three finalists (none with UC experience and two from private universities) would be able to step in as quickly and as ably as we needed in our dramatically deteriorating budget circumstance. I suspended the search, much to the consternation of three recruitment advisory committee faculty who strongly favored one candidate, and I appointed Enrique Lavernia (then College of Engineering dean) for a three-year term as provost. The three faculty members brought to our Academic Senate a resolution criticizing my actions—variously described by Senate members at the April 14 meeting as an "outrage," "a slap in the face," "insulting," "rinky-dink," "horrifying" and showing "contempt" for the faculty (*Dateline UC Davis*, April 17, 2008)—and demanding changes in the search process for administrative leaders. The resolution was unanimously approved that afternoon and sent to UC President Robert Dynes in a stiffly worded letter.

Another vote of no confidence seemed headed my way. Pre-emptively, I moved up by a few months my planned announcement that I would step down as chancellor at the end of the campus's 2008-09 centennial year. Not a consequential change in timing—not a thorny decision avoided—but nonetheless an action taken with a possible vote weighing on my mind. I didn't want to repeat that agonizing experience if I didn't have to, not with my tenure as chancellor coming to a close.

IN PROPORTION

My views on no-confidence votes aren't entirely objective. I don't think they can be. But they do echo a statement in a "con" ballot argument signed by 14 faculty members: *"The use of a mail ballot of the faculty should be done under exceptional circumstances and faculty should exercise this privilege with care."*

(The ballot statement was submitted by Zuhair A. Munir, Robert L. Powell, Melvin R. Ramey, Ann E. Orel, Jay Lund, Thomas M. Young, Alan P. Jackman, Bruce Hartsough, James F. Shackelford, Anthony Wexler, Jean-Jacques Chattot, Matthew Farrens, Jeannie Darby, Miguel Marino).

At UC Davis, it takes just 50 signatures to trigger a Senate-wide vote on any issue—a provision of Senate Bylaw 17 that has been in place since 1969.

The campus was a different place in 1969—just a little more than 13,000 students (compared to today's 35,000), 1,700 faculty and other academics (4,100 today), and 3,600 staff (17,400 today). Fifty faculty signatures back then represented a much greater proportion of the Senate faculty than they do today—signatures that now could essentially be gathered on a free lunch hour.

Perhaps it's time—nearly 50 years later—for our Senate to revisit the 50-signature trigger. I do hope so. Perhaps a more proportional number would better ensure the thoughtful, representative deliberations on exceptional issues that I expect the original Bylaw 17 writers had in mind.

But, more than anything, I hope our faculty and administrators will always be good-faith partners—willing to listen, to negotiate, to work cooperatively to resolve issues.

And, when most needed, willing to give one another the benefit of the doubt.

The 1995 Politics and Principle of Affirmative Action

Every segment of the institution believes firmly in the use of race. I want them to unleash all their creative capacity to find new ways to achieve diversity.
—UC REGENT WARD CONNERLY AT JULY 20, 1995, UC BOARD OF
   REGENTS MEETING

Any action now to dismantle our diversity programs would be premature and against the best interests of the University of California.
—UC PRESIDENT JACK PELTASON AT JULY 20, 1995, UC BOARD OF
   REGENTS MEETING

This is one of the saddest days the university has encountered. There was no urgency, no reason to force the university to take a stand.
—LIEUTENANT GOVERNOR AND UC REGENT GRAY DAVIS AT
   JULY 20, 1995, UC BOARD OF REGENTS MEETING

THE PARTISAN POLITICAL TRAIN HAD LONG LEFT THE STATION.

California Gov. Pete Wilson, who'd persuasively won reelection in 1994 after championing popular anti-immigrant Proposition 187, now had grander aspirations. He was positioning himself to be president of the United States. And opposition to affirmative action—a politically powerful wedge issue—was to be his ticket to the White House.

The University of California's affirmative action programs provided the perfect high-profile platform to energize his campaign. Among the first universities to adopt diversity programs some 30 years before, UC would make national news if its Board of Regents (which included Wilson) upended them. And, given UC's constitutional autonomy, such a decision to end consideration of race, ethnicity and gender in student admissions, hiring and contracting couldn't be overturned by the state's Legislature.

It would be a sharp and shocking change in direction.

"For three decades, most of what Regents, governors and legislators wanted to know from the administration was when minority enrollment figures were going to improve at UC," Patricia Pelfrey writes in her book *Entrepreneurial President: Richard Atkinson and the University of California, 1995-2003.* UC (and California State University, as well) were expected to enroll undergraduate student bodies that mirrored the racial, ethnic, cultural and economic characteristics of the state's public high school students. It was

105

an expectation strongly embraced by the university, where diversity was seen to be an important educational asset and where providing access was considered a public university's responsibility.

Gov. Pete Wilson, an affirmative action opponent, listens to the Rev. Jesse Jackson urge continuation of UC's policies. (Photo: Associated Press, p. 10 of Entrepreneurial President by Patricia A. Pelfrey)

Governor Wilson had an earnest and eloquent ally in pushing for a reversal of this policy—Ward Connerly, a Sacramento African-American businessman and longtime friend whom he'd appointed to the UC Board of Regents in 1993.

Ward felt successful minorities were stigmatized by affirmative action—by the assumption they owed their success to an unfair boost tied to the color of their skin. And he was sympathetic to the complaints of a white San Diego family whose son had been passed over for admission to UC San Diego's medical school while minority students with lower grades and test scores had gotten in. He carried those concerns to his fellow regents.

"Make no mistake," Ward told the board at its January 1995 meeting. "We would not be here today as basically an integrated society if we had not embarked on affirmative action in 1965. I can't tell you the humiliation of drinking from a fountain that says 'Colored Only.' But I tell you with every fiber of my being that what we're doing is inequitable to certain people. I want something in its place that is fair."

UC President Jack Peltason persuaded the regents to delay action till mid-1995 so they could be better informed about UC's affirmative action programs (which supplemented academic criteria with consideration of geography, race, ethnicity, gender and special talents), and so he could complete a review of current practices (practices that assured every academically eligible undergraduate applicant a spot at UC, but not always at the preferred campus). If problems were found, he pledged to fix them.

At the same time, signatures were being gathered (due Feb. 21, 1996) for a proposed November 1996 ballot initiative (later named Proposition 209) that would ban race- and gender-based preferences in state hiring, contracting and college admissions. Jack told the governor and Ward that it would take at least that long for UC's Academic Senate to devise alternate admissions criteria. Why not wait till the initiative's outcome was known, he urged, rather than embroil the university in such a divisive issue that the state's voters would likely ultimately decide.

But no ground was given. A vote to end race and gender preferences would be taken at the regents' July 1995 meeting.

As *The Sacramento Bee* later editorialized ("UC: The politics came first," July 22, 1995), "Instead of using outside auditors to get reliable data—data particularly on what the alternatives were and what they would produce—instead of waiting to consult with the new president they will have to hire in the coming weeks, [the regents] marched to the pace of the only thing that required the haste with which they acted: the timetable of Gov. Pete Wilson's presidential campaign."

TUMULTUOUS MARATHON MEETING

In my 15 years as chancellor, I've never seen a UC Board of Regents meeting more tumultuous than the regents' July 20, 1995, gathering.

The scene that Thursday changed sporadically from chaotic to monotonous, from star-charged to politically charged, from exhilarating to depressing.

Upwards of 800 members of the public and 300 members of the news media had crowded UC San Francisco's Laurel Heights campus to attend what would become a marathon 12-hour meeting disrupted by protests and by a room-clearing bomb threat. For six hours, the regents listened to testimony from more than 60 public officials and members of the public—including the Rev. Jesse Jackson, Assemblyman Willie Brown and Governor Wilson (attending his first UC board meeting in three years). And for another six hours, they heatedly debated among themselves Ward's proposals to end the use of race- and gender-based preferences.

Finally, after 8 p.m., the regents, by close votes—14-10 (with one abstention) on admissions and 15-10 on hiring and contracting—

The Rev. Jesse Jackson was trailed by more than 150 demonstrators and a throng of reporters and photographers as he arrived at UCSF for the regents meeting. (Photo: Neil Michel/Axiom)

took actions opposed by UC's president and vice presidents, all nine chancellors and UC's faculty, student and alumni leaders.

We were stunned. We'd felt that somehow it'd be pulled out in the end, that consensus-builder Regent Roy Brophy would find sufficient support for his compromise proposal. Roy wanted the board to appoint a task force to consider equitable alternatives to race and gender preferences while waiting for the ballot initiative's fate to be decided. And he appeared to have the votes until Wilson reportedly pressed regents to withdraw their support.

"I was a big fund-raiser for him many years ago, and he's still a friend of mine, but I do not appreciate the vote going the way it did," Roy later told *Sacramento Bee* reporter James Richardson ("Political axing of affirmative action galls UC's Brophy," *The Sacramento Bee*, July 29, 1995).

Regent Roy Brophy (Photo: UC Davis)

Roy was my close friend and I never admired him more than through this crisis. I watched him become increasingly exasperated at this meeting, his flushed face frequently lighting up during the discussion. He was certain that the University of California had lost a significant piece of its soul on July 20, 1995.

That next morning, Roy startled the regents and everyone else in attendance by asking to address the board as a private citizen. He left the regents' table and walked around to the public speakers' microphone. With sometimes shaky passion, he rebuked his colleagues: "This board cannot operate this university unilaterally. Your board managed to circumvent the chancellors. You managed to circumvent the faculty, and you managed to circumvent the students."

That five-minute speech was, many said, Roy's finest hour. He knew he was exactly sideways with his close friend, Governor Wilson. But he felt he couldn't stand down.

A few months later, Roy joined me at the Oct. 12 Affirmative Action Day teach-in on the Quad. And, at a Nov. 14 shared-governance forum sponsored by the Davis Faculty Association, he called the regents' decision "the most flagrant violation of the rights of the faculty that I ever saw and hope never to see again."

OUTREACH

While the regents took away race and gender as supplemental admissions criteria, they adopted a last-minute amendment to their resolutions that endorsed the value and continued pursuit of diversity. In particular, they advocated outreach that would increase eligibility of disadvantaged students "who demonstrate economic or social need." And they invited proposals for increased funding for such outreach efforts.

A window was still open.

New UC President Dick Atkinson (appointed barely four weeks after the regents' vote) and all the chancellors took that pro-diversity amendment very seriously (though a few regents privately wondered if some regents approved it only to get the necessary votes on the main resolutions).

Regardless, that amendment gave some hope and consolation to UC's administrators as we focused on developing new strategies and tactics to develop and encourage diversity— strategies we'd strongly felt should have been tested before abandoning current practices that, despite problems, had had major demonstrated successes. Diversity was too great a strength—in the classroom, in the residence hall, around the decision-making table—to lose. It was part and parcel of our pursuit of the highest standards of excellence.

Those who knew me well understood my strong personal commitment to this issue. My parents were educated only to the eighth grade. Without special help, I never would have finished high school, let alone college. I didn't want others, through no fault of their own, to miss out on a merited opportunity for higher education while we figured out our new circumstance.

The new undergraduate admissions policy was to take effect in January 1997 but for practical reasons was postponed by President Atkinson until fall 1998—a miscom-

Chants, speeches and intense discussions about new rules for admissions, contracting and hiring marked the Oct. 12, 1995, Affirmative Action Day at UC Davis. At its peak, the event drew about 400 students as well as faculty and staff members. UC Regents Roy Brophy and Ralph Carmona joined me during the morning teach-in on the Quad. Later Regent Carmona addressed a large crowd during the noon-time rally sponsored by the Coalition for Social Justice. (Photo: Neil Michel/Axiom)

municated decision that nearly got Dick fired. A conciliatory compromise of spring 1998 was ultimately accepted by a publicly irate governor and 10 regents who had called for a special meeting to review Dick's performance. Another crisis was averted— while Dick ended up getting the added time (till fall 1998) the university needed to admit its first full undergraduate class under the regents' new rules.

Camping out on Mrak Hall's north apron, students fasted on a rotational basis for 10 days in November 1995 to protest changes in the university's affirmative-action policies. (Photo: Neil Michel/Axiom)

NEW APPROACHES

At the board's January 15, 1998, meeting, Dick announced a new outreach initiative to "improve the educational experience and preparation of K-12 students on a scale and scope never attempted before." More focus, more funding, more intensified personal outreach efforts by the regents, the president, the chancellors—all recommended by the Regents Outreach Task Force (a group on which I was privileged to serve).

Regents Ward Connerly (right) and Robert Morrison (middle) listen to discussion before the board voted to rescind SP-1 at its May 2001 meeting. (Photo: Associated Press, p. 90 of Entrepreneurial President by Patricia A. Pelfrey)

At that meeting, I had the chance to tell regents about UC Davis' expanded educational outreach effort and our initiative partners—CSU-Sacramento, the Los Rios Community College District, and the Sacramento, Grant and Del Paso School Districts. Our partnership involved not just our high school feeder schools, but the feeder schools of the feeder schools.

In particular, our "Reservation for College" program reached out to fourth grade students and their parents with a plan for college—a plan describing each step to be taken from the fourth grade forward to achieve admission to UC and to successfully complete college work. We knew we needed to start early to help these kids stay on track.

Other campuses were pursuing their own initiatives, giving UC several strategies to consider and evaluate as we shaped a new approach to diversity.

"The challenge of educational equity is so immense—and solutions so crucial to the future of this state—that we can't be into and out of this business of K-12 outreach as the enthusiasm of chancellors and regents and governors and legislators waxes and wanes," I told the regents. "To even hope to apply more than a Band-Aid, to truly bring about systemic reform, we must make a sustained commitment of our attention and resources. We have to commit for the long term, because this is a long-term project.

Father Keith B. Kenny Elementary School children, late 1990s (Photo: Neil Michel/Axiom)

"How can we look into the faces of these elementary school children and do less? They—and their younger brothers and sisters—deserve the same kinds of opportunities that have blessed all of us."

Along with expanded outreach, the university (led by the faculty) developed more comprehensive admissions criteria and implemented a more holistic review of every student applicant's accomplishments and potential. A new "Eligibility in the Local Context" plan guaranteed admission to students in the top 4 percent (later expanded to 9 percent) of their California high school class. The university pared its Scholastic Aptitude Test requirements, pointing to high school grade point average as the best predictor of college success. And UC spent many millions more on financial aid, benefiting (but not targeting) underrepresented minorities.

TWO DECADES LATER

I'd like to say we figured it out over the past 20-some years—that we now know how to unquestionably measure merit and dispense educational opportunity, to compose an entering class of precisely the most deserving and most promising students. A class that is broadly accomplished and richly diverse.

But, of course, that's naïve. Merit still eludes definitive measurement (GPAs and test scores simply aren't adequate). Some states (including ours) have approved ballot initiatives prohibiting consideration of race in college admissions. And the courts—all the way to the U.S. Supreme Court—have offered differing and inconclusive judgments about the validity of race as a factor in admissions.

In 2013, then-UC President Mark Yudof submitted, with UC's 10 chancellors, a "friend of the court" brief to the U.S. Supreme Court in support of the University of Michigan in Schuette v. Coalition to Defend Affirmative Action. (The case challenged Michigan's Proposal 2, which, like California's Proposition 209, prohibits consideration of race in college admissions.)

"The University of California is the nation's largest highly-selective university system in the nation's most populous and diverse state," the brief stated. "We feel it is incumbent upon us to inform the Court, and the nation, about our ceaseless efforts to enroll a student body that is reflective of our diverse citizenry. We would hope, after 16 years of operating under Proposition 209, that we could report more success. But without the judicious use of tools such as affirmative action we have been unable to do so."

In a narrow 6-2 ruling the following spring, the Supreme Court upheld Michigan's voter-approved ban but took no position on the constitutionality of race considerations in admissions decisions.

That ruling prompted an April 25, 2014, opinion piece by new UC President Janet Napolitano in *The Washington Post*.

"For nearly two decades, we have served as a laboratory of innovation for race-blind strategies to promote diversity on our campuses," she wrote. "We will continue these vital efforts. But as long as the university is prohibited from considering all of an applicant's characteristics, we will be doing so with one arm tied tightly behind our backs."

Race should never be the only consideration, she wrote, but neither should it be singled out for prohibition.

She agreed with dissenting Supreme Court Justice Sonia Sotomayor that race matters.

It still matters. And yet we're directed to achieve diversity as if it didn't—with our eyes closed and with that one arm tied tightly behind our backs.

But we're trying. And that matters, too.

▶ **http://escholarship.org/uc/ucdavischancelloremeritus_books**

STATEMENT BY THE PRESIDENT AND CHANCELLORS OF THE UNIVERSITY OF CALIFORNIA • JULY 21, 1995

A diverse student population is an essential component of a quality educational environment. Within the University of California, we have been governed by a 1988 Regental policy which mandates that we enroll a student population that encompasses the cultural diversity of the State of California. That policy has served the University and the state well, and we remain firmly committed to the principles it embodies.

The action of the Board of Regents at its July 20, 1995, meeting eliminates the use of race, ethnicity and gender as supplemental criteria in the admissions process. This will unfortunately make it more difficult for our campuses to achieve the diversity that is essential for the future excellence of the University and the stability and welfare of our society. However, we pledge to continue our efforts to serve all populations in California, working within the new guidelines of economic and social disadvantage, and in conformance with state and federal mandates.

We applaud the proposal to enhance outreach as a means of increasing the number of ethnic minority students eligible to enroll in the University. We pledge to retain those elements of affirmative action that have proven of such great value to our institution, including open employment searches.

We shall use every means available to us to accelerate our pursuit of the twin goals of excellence and diversity.

UC President Jack W. Peltason
Berkeley Campus Chancellor Chang-Lin Tien
Davis Campus Chancellor Larry N. Vanderhoef
Irvine Campus Chancellor Laurel L. Wilkening
Los Angeles Campus Chancellor Charles E. Young
Riverside Campus Chancellor Raymond L. Orbach
San Diego Campus Chancellor Richard C. Atkinson
San Francisco Campus Chancellor Joseph B. Martin
Santa Barbara Campus Chancellor Henry T. Yang
Santa Cruz Campus Chancellor Karl S. Pister

College-bound Fourth-graders

That sunny 1999 day at Father Keith B. Kenny Elementary School in Sacramento's Oak Park neighborhood, I made a pledge to an excited group of fourth-graders. The pledge was simple enough: If you study hard and if you make grades good enough to be admitted to UC Davis, then the university will pay the equivalent of your university fees and tuition.

I handed out my business cards to Kenny Elementary School students, saying, "Tell your parents that, if they have any questions along the way, you have a friend at UC Davis they can call." At right is Early Academic Outreach's Shelley Davis. (Photo: Neil Michel/Axiom)

Looking out that day, over that sea of bright young faces, none of us knew how many or if any of them would see it through and arrive on our doorstep. It was a gamble.

To provide help along the way, we created a program called Reservation for College. Its job was to assist them on their journey. Then we waited. And we all waited together. The teachers waited. The parents waited. Our partners, the Sacramento City Unified School District, the Del Paso Heights School District and our alumni, who contributed to a $1 million endowment for this purpose, waited. One of our truly pivotal partners, Principal Mertie Shelby, waited. The community waited. We all waited together to see what would happen.

Teachers and university staff, most notably from our Early Academic Outreach Program, continued to work with what were now no longer fourth-graders, encouraging them along the way. Perhaps most importantly, their parents continued to reinforce the message that college was a realistic and obtainable goal.

The Reservation for College curriculum demonstrated the importance of hard work, perseverance and resilience. The lessons helped to instill in children a stronger sense of control over their own destinies and increase their motivation and willingness to take on challenging tasks.

To reinforce students' confidence and focus on learning as a process, many of the activities required students to work in cooperative learning groups. They solved tasks together. Through it all they continued to grow and to progress academically, intellectually, spiritually and physically.

Of course the question remained: Would we see a difference? Nine years is, after all, a long time. People move. Family circumstances change. The challenges of life can impose enormous obstacles to overcome. It is a daunting task to set out with a goal in mind and to pursue that goal with focus and resolve. None of us knew if we would be back together nearly a decade later. No one had really tried this before.

We all are familiar with the concept of acorns. You plant an acorn, give it sun and soil and water and hope that one day it will grow into a mighty oak tree. It's a simple but applicable concept. Would our acorns germinate and grow?

On Sept. 21, 2007, we knew the answer. Five students from Father Keith B. Kenny School, all of whom were there on that sunny day nine years earlier, were about to begin their studies at UC Davis. They had fulfilled the pledge. And it was a cause for celebration. We saluted them (and their families) that day at their former elementary school. The Sacramento High School Band performed and the Kenny Choir sang a "Reservation for College" song specially composed when this academic prep program was launched. I couldn't have been prouder of our five new students or more optimistic about the new fourth-graders in attendance. I quickly learned you didn't ask them *if* they were going to college, but *where!*

Newly admitted UC Davis student Porcha Chambers reacts as she shakes my hand during a Sept. 21, 2007, ceremony honoring her and four other students in our inaugural Reservation for College class. (Photo: Karin Higgins/UC Davis)

(Over the years, Reservation for College served thousands of students in more than 15 elementary schools in the Elk Grove, Del Paso Heights [now Twin Rivers], Sacramento and Woodland school districts. But state budget cuts to academic preparation programs forced cutbacks, leading to the eventual ending of Reservation for College after more than a decade. Conversations are beginning about possibly bringing back some of its components.)

Supremely Disappointed

*Unlike Groucho Marx, we didn't say "Those are our principles,
and if you don't like them...well, we have others."*
—BRUCE WOLK, FORMER UC DAVIS LAW DEAN

OUR LAW SCHOOL STUDENTS HAD WORKED VERY HARD FOR MONTHS IN
advance to entice U.S. Supreme Court Justice Harry Blackmun to be their 1993 commencement speaker.

They were thrilled when he said "yes," encouraged to accept the invitation by his former law clerk Vikram Amar, who had since joined the
UC Davis law faculty.

But, just 12 days before the ceremony, Blackmun informed the law school that he would not come if the campus permitted television reporters to cover his speech. Unhappy with "sound bite" coverage, he would only agree to have TV reporters in the audience if their stations agreed to broadcast his remarks in their entirety.

You can imagine how crushed our law school grads were to have this last-minute monkey-wrench thrown into the works.

As a public university, we could not agree to Blackmun's demands.

**Supreme Court Justice Harry
Blackmun (Courtesy photo)**

We issued a news release announcing that Blackmun had withdrawn and expressing disappointment at his decision. I was the bearer of the bad news in that release, explaining that barring any element of the news media from a public ceremony at a public university was not, in our view, appropriate.

At the 11th hour, U.S. Supreme Court Justice Harry Blackmun withdrew as law school commencement speaker over demands we could not meet.

In the emotion of the moment, my decision was not a popular one for many of our soon-to-be law school grads (nor for *The California Aggie*, which editorialized that "The lack of planning and flexibility on the behalf of the administration to accommodate Blackmun makes it hard to believe that they realized the significance and positive impact his speech would have for the law school").

In their desperation to salvage Blackmun as their speaker, law students the next day faxed an "off-the-record and confidential" proposal to our five area television stations, asking them to agree not to excerpt his remarks.

As you would expect, our students got a lesson in the First Amendment—and in what "off the record" means. Television officials were unanimous in their refusal to acquiesce to the students' request, saying it amounted to prior restraint—a form of censorship.

One TV news director quoted in a *Sacramento Bee* article reporting the students' appeal had this to say: "There's absolutely no conceivable circumstance under which [we] would agree to those conditions. It's an outrageous requirement…. Maybe these law students should review the First Amendment."

A typical law school commencement at Recreation Hall (now the Pavilion). Since 2010, law graduates have walked across the stage of the Mondavi Center's Jackson Hall to receive their degrees. (Photo: UC Davis)

Said another: "There's no way I will agree to modify my fundamental rights so they can have a speaker. Blackmun should take out the Constitution and take a quick read. He's trying to stifle the freedom of the press by stopping me from doing my job or controlling the way I do it."

With the clock ticking, alternate proposals were feverishly floated to law school Dean Bruce Wolk and Associate Dean Rex Perschbacher:

"What about moving graduation to an off-campus site like the Unitarian Church or the Stonegate Country Club?" Nope; that wouldn't solve the problem.

"How about conferring the degrees publicly and then completing the ceremony at another spot where Blackmun is waiting and broadcast reporters are restricted?" Again, problematic.

"Well, isn't commencement really a private event since tickets are required?" Sorry, no; tickets are only required because seating is limited.

Even if, taking Groucho Marx's cue, we had abandoned our public-university principles, neither Bruce nor Rex believe Blackmun would have come. They're both convinced that, as commencement drew nearer, the 84-year-old justice was looking for a way out of his cross-country commitment. The last-minute no-broadcast-media stipulation was a handy way to pull the plug. Law school registrar Nicole Waterman, who had been in "constant contact" with Blackmun's staff about commencement details, shares that belief.

Of course there wasn't a way to call his bluff.

But I've read with interest since then (in the 2011 book *Justices and Journalists: The U.S. Supreme Court and the Media* by Richard Davis) that Blackmun "was the first justice to dramatically break from the no-television interview tradition by giving repeated television interviews during his last decade or so on the Court." (Blackmun served on the Court from 1970 to 1994.)

On the other hand, Davis' book also notes that Blackmun highlighted certain sections of his personal copy of the American Society of Newspaper Editors code of ethics, suggesting he believed that reporters "had at least occasionally treated the code as merely aspirational." And Vik Amar, the UC Davis law professor who'd clerked for Blackmun in 1989-90, believes the justice was genuinely concerned about the emotive effect of out-of-context video snippets because he was the author of the controversial *Roe v. Wade* decision.

But no matter. Whatever the intent of his 11th-hour broadcast-media stipulation, we had no choice but to say no.

Much as I was sure our course was the right one, I *was* surprised to see the degree to which our decision was applauded by the news media.

The president of the Radio-Television News Directors Association wrote to me after reading in *The New York Times* about the Blackmun episode. "On behalf of electronic journalists everywhere," he wrote, "thank you for placing First Amendment values above your desire to schedule a prominent speaker."

New York Newsday went so far as to suggest that "maybe [I'm] the one who ought to be on the Supreme Court." Now that was an amusing thought.

The *Legal Times* in Washington, D.C., also weighed in. "Hopefully, UC Davis will start a trend. The justices have been encouraged in their silly requests to bar cameras by host organizations that quake in their boots for fear of angering their guests. The only way the justices' habit will be cured is for more groups to decide they won't cave in."

That habit wasn't soon broken, though. Four years later, Supreme Court Justice Sandra Day O'Connor insisted that recording devices be banned if she were to address law school graduates at the University of Montana. The law dean consented, thrilled to have landed her as the school's commencement speaker. I was heartened to hear, though, that he later got dressed down by the university's journalism dean.

Today's U.S. Supreme Court media policy is, well, open to interpretation. According to a public information specialist there, "The media arrangements for a Justice's appearance are worked out on a case-by-case basis and depend upon factors such as the nature of the event, the preferences of the Justice, and the practices of the organization hosting the event. If broadcast coverage is permitted, however, there are generally no requirements that the event be aired in its entirety."

Gracious. Sounds like it may still be wise to have a good back-up plan.

With the help of an alum, we were able to secure a former (now current) California governor, Edmund G. "Jerry" Brown Jr., as our pinch-hitting keynote speaker, and his remarks were warmly received.

I wish I could say the same about my own. Student speaker Jared Moses—now a Los Angeles Superior Court judge—preceded me at the podium, bitingly ref-

When Supreme Court Justice Blackmun unexpectedly canceled, former (now current) California Gov. Jerry Brown (center) pinch-hit as the law school's keynote commencement speaker, to the immense relief of former law Dean Bruce Wolk (right) and me. (Photo: UC Davis)

erencing the kerfuffle with a string of such satirical movie titles as "When Harry Met Larry," "The Dean Vanishes" and "You're a Good Man, Jerry Brown." He ended his remarks by passing around a Costco-sized container of sour gumballs to his fellow graduates—one of whom told me "You're disgusting!" as she crossed the stage to receive her diploma.

Definitely a tough audience that afternoon. But I could understand their disappointment. They'd lost a Supreme Court Justice as their keynote speaker just days before their graduation. And they were about to jump into a terribly tight job market, thanks to the early '90s recession. Truly a moment for sour-gumball reflection.

Some 20 years later, Jared—now Judge Moses—explains his gumball sharing in a kinder and gentler way: "There was a group of us who chewed tons of the stuff during law school. In honor of that, I passed out the gum to signify the sourness and sweetness of our law school experience, analogizing to the bitter herbs and sweet charoset served at the Passover Seder."

Though without as colorful a prop, I hoped Jared and his fellow graduates would embrace my heartfelt message that day: "And so, graduates, remember this. Values and principles of behavior are your most important possessions. They mark your path. They mark the path of the organizations with which you will associate. Value them as you do your closest friendships, for they are your friends. And never, ever, give up your friends."

Somehow I just know they've held fast to their ideals. That's what we've come to know about our law students. What they learn within the classrooms and hallways of Martin Luther King Hall they're bound to carry with them for life.

An Unmatched, Top-Notch Staff

Over the years I could tell the difference between those who said they supported staff and those who actually believed and meant it.
—DENNIS SHIMEK, SENIOR ASSOCIATE VICE CHANCELLOR
    FOR HUMAN RESOURCES, 1966-2007

I MUST HAVE LOOKED LIKE QUITE THE ODDITY.

People were hurriedly passing by, their chins to their chests and their arms wrapped around themselves for warmth, rushed along by a chilly north wind. The thought of stopping to sit on an outdoor bench wasn't even remotely on the mind of anyone who had to be out that day.

But there I sat on a brand new bench by the Heitman Staff Learning Center, hardly minding the cold—and thinking gratefully about the Staff Assembly leaders who'd dedicated it to me just a few weeks before. It had rained hard on dedication day (March 14, 2012), so this was my first chance to give the bench a try and to read its inscription: "With our gratitude to Chancellor Emeritus Larry N. Vanderhoef. We thank you for your support of UC Davis staff and your commitment to their personal growth and development...."

Former Staff Assembly Chair Rob Kerner and I enjoyed a chat on the special bench that Rob, on behalf of the assembly, dedicated to me in March 2012. (Photo: Stephen McKone/UC Davis)

That gratitude is reciprocated—a hundred-fold.

I'd been at several universities before arriving at UC Davis in 1984, and I'd served on dozens of universities' accreditation review teams over my 40-year career. One campus always stood out. Nowhere—nowhere—have I found staff more accomplished, more dedicated, than our own.

Staff truly are a special mark of distinction for UC Davis.

It didn't take me long to learn that. My first public remarks as the campus's new executive vice chancellor were made to Staff Assembly. I'd said then what the staff had already demonstrated—they were absolutely indispensable to a campus this size and played an essential role in keeping the university operating smoothly.

Just returned from fighting a 2003 Southern California fire, UC Davis firefighters Cess Mercado and Terry Weisser shared their experiences with me. (Photo: Debbie Aldridge/UC Davis)

When I became chancellor, the complexity of the staff's collective work became clearer to me as we interacted more. With an astounding panoply of talents, they make the university run. Just think of all that's required to support our academic community—the equivalent of a large corporation but with unique teaching, research and service responsibilities (including a medical center and an animal hospital), and with complex, around-the-clock city functions added (police, fire, housing, utilities, water, waste management, parking, etc.). Heavy lifting, without a doubt—and done remarkably well by members of our staff.

They're the glue between faculty and students; the backbone for everything the campus undertakes; the institutional historians; the continuity as administrators change, faculty depart and students graduate; and, not insignificantly, the keepers of the campus's culture.

A FEELING OF FAMILY

For reasons I don't fully understand, staff here feel that the campus is home, is family—not just a career stop along the way.

There are many day-to-day indicators of that sense of connection, that sense of "family"—for example, the waves of greeting as the drivers of Facilities department vehicles pass each other on the road, the clusters of staff walking the Arboretum together on their lunch hours, the departmental potlucks and ice cream socials, the Redwood Grove baby showers, the noon-hour gatherings to watch the latest British-broadcast episode of "Downton Abbey," a Management Service Officer's hand-knitted socks to welcome new staff and faculty, the chocolates and flowers presented to counselors by grateful graduating students, and the remarkably generous (and anonymous) donation of vacation time to co-workers on catastrophic medical leave who've exhausted their own leave balances.

Perhaps most remarkable is the staff's predisposition to collaborate rather than compete—a characteristic of this campus since its earliest days. That valuing of shared success and teamwork gives UC Davis a distinct advantage and makes the greatest gains possible.

Staff members are also exceptionally loyal. Most retire with more than two decades of service. And many achieve membership in the UC Davis Quarter Century Club (an annual gathering of employees who have served the campus for at least 25 years).

Faculty members who serve the usual five-year term as department chairs are particularly grateful for staff's seasoned wisdom since they depend heavily on their much-longer-serving Management Service Officers to show them the administrative ropes—to essentially teach them how to be a chair.

MULTIPLE FAMILY GENERATIONS

For decades, multiple generations of longstanding families in our surrounding communities—principally Dixon, Winters, Woodland and Davis—have contributed steadfastly and significantly to the campus' success. Mothers, daughters, fathers, sons, aunts, uncles, even an occasional grandchild!

Edie Silva—the "mom" part of a mother/father/daughter trio—I knew and appreciated from my first second here. She ran the Chancellor's Office. If you had to figure out how to do something, she had the wisest counsel (and the expert follow through), and served the campus for 26 years (all the way back to Chancellors Mrak and Meyer) before retiring. Her husband, Milt (a student here in the 1940s), worked for the Department of Plant Pathology, contributing 35 years of service before he retired (with almost as many years volunteering—for example, umpiring baseball, keeping the men's basketball scorebook, and moving the sideline markers or running the scoreboard at football games).

I also came to know their daughter Darlene ("Dar") Hunter, who is senior director of our Undergraduate Admissions Office and, with more than 40 years of service now, has eclipsed even her parents' longstanding record.

But Dar's contributions far exceed a simple tally of years (besides, to be fully accurate, you'd have to start counting from her childhood, when she was drafted as the baseball team's bat girl and accompanied her dad to football, basketball and track and field events).

She's also a perfect example of that figurative "family" notion of staff.

Darlene Hunter (center) and her father, Milt Silva, and mother, Edie Silva, have contributed more than 100 years of service as UC Davis staff members. They're pictured here at Dar's 25-year-pin celebration. (Courtesy photo)

For instance, for years she was the Department of Military Science's chief judge for its annual Chili Cook Off—a wonderful chance, she'd said, to meet UC Davis colleagues in a non-work setting and to give back to the campus. She's a true blue (and gold) fan of intercollegiate athletics—an original TeamAggie member and former president, a member (and then chair) of the Cal Aggie Athletics Hall of Fame Committee for more than 18 years, and a perennial season ticket holder for football and for women's basketball (which presents an award in her name to a player best demonstrating persistence).

Like so many UC Davis staff members, Dar was drawn by UC Davis' "sense of unity, family and stability." And, like others, she's had opportunities to go elsewhere. "But I've never wanted to leave. Everything I believe in is what this place is about."

A PLACE TO LEARN

Angela Taggart, currently a Workers' Compensation specialist on campus, represents the third generation of her family to serve UC Davis. Her grandmother, Marie Gallardo, retired after 20-plus years in Payroll. Her mother, Diane Sires, got her start here as a student, ultimately re-

Working the food line was a favorite assignment at our annual Thank Goodness for Staff barbecue. Here I'm serving Jan Conroy, director of Editorial/ Design. (Photo: Debbie Aldridge/UC Davis)

tiring from the Department of Land, Air and Water Resources with 29 years of service. Her father, Ray Sires, served as an officer and detective in our Police Department in the 1970s. And her brother, Jeff, as well as a great uncle and two second cousins, also chose to work here.

Staff Assembly presented its Citations for Excellence at a Chancellor's Residence reception in May 2009. Pictured here is UC Davis Extension's Northern California Training Academy Team, whose members pitched in (over an 18-month period) to cover for five of their co-workers on maternity leave. From left: Amy Spakosky, Nancy Hafer and baby Ginger, Hilary Wilkoff, Christie Karlstad, Ann Gibson, Jennifer Davis, Kristi Smith, Melanie Schindell and Christine Altavilla. Not pictured: Grace Barajas, Chris Juvinall and Ken Ly. (Photo: Kathy Keatley Garvey/UC Davis)

"We have all been proud to work on campus," Angela says. "From the time I was a little girl, I can remember my mom and dad and grandmother talking about their work on campus and what a great and exciting place it is to work, learn and meet new people. They always said that the university takes care of its employees by offering great pay, benefits, retirement and educational opportunities."

I know it's gotten tougher for the university to offer the pay and benefits it knows our employees deserve. And I know growing workloads continue to be a challenge. But I also see our staff remaining positive and hardworking.

Especially important to me is ensuring that they continue to have opportunities to advance in their careers. "Training and education should be available for all who want it," I'd told Staff Assembly in 1984.

Twenty-five years later, as I prepared to step down as chancellor, I was asked how gifts in my honor might be directed. The answer was easy—to a new scholarship fund to help staff members continue their education (and to help students study abroad).

I look forward each spring to presenting the Larry N. Vanderhoef Staff Scholarship to an aspiring applicant selected by Staff Assembly for "outstanding demonstration and commitment to community service, work, self-improvement, school, financial need and other worthy merits."

The 2003 UC Davis-American Heart Association 5K Walk/Run drew together several hundred staff and faculty (including a Chancellor's office team) to raise funds for heart research, education and public outreach—a cause close to my heart because my mother died at age 52 of a heart attack. (Photo: Debbie Aldridge/ UC Davis)

That presentation is a small but personally very meaningful way for me to continue to signal my abiding respect and deep gratitude for our staff.

They've been part of my extended family for three decades. And they've been an indispensable contributor to UC Davis' success for more than a century.

That's what I'll be thinking about, and appreciating, whenever I sit on that very special bench.

LARRY N. VANDERHOEF STAFF SCHOLARSHIP RECIPIENTS

Below are the staff members (to date) who have been awarded a Larry N. Vanderhoef Staff Scholarship.

2011-2012

MAYRA LLAMAS

Program Manager, Student Recruitment and Retention Center

Scholarship purpose: Doctorate in Educational Leadership program, UC Davis/Sonoma State University

2012-2013

IOANA ENE

Library Assistant III, Blaisdell Medical Library

Scholarship purpose: Master of Library and Information Science program, San Jose State Universityy

2013-2014

WENDY ANNE STOLTZ

Development Analyst, Graduate School of Management

Scholarship purpose: MBA program, Mills College

KELLY MARIE COLE

Academic Advising Coordinator, Student Housing

Scholarship purpose: Doctorate in Educational Leadership program, UC Davis/Sonoma State University

2014-2015

SHAUNA STEWART

Teacher Education Assistant, School of Education

Scholarship purpose: Master of Library and Information Science program, San Jose State University

The Value of *We*—Not *I*—Leadership

You're presiding over a process. You're not presiding over an organization like I did in the Marine Corps where I told people what to do and they did it. You influence the direction, you influence the flow—or you can make a mess out of it.
—JAMES H. MEYER, UC DAVIS CHANCELLOR, 1969-87, AND EARLY
    LEADER IN ADAPTING MANAGEMENT THEORY AND TECHNIQUES
    TO HIGHER EDUCATION

THEY WERE PUZZLED. IMPRESSED, MAYBE, WITH THE MAGNANIMITY OF MY suggestion, but definitely puzzled.

"But how can you get ahead if you don't get the credit?" asked the group of Cuarto residence halls students.

My quarterly brown bag updates—initiated during the early 1990s as we coped with severe budget cuts—gave faculty, staff and students a regular chance to meet with me (and other campus leaders) to ask questions, raise concerns and hear what was on my mind. (Photo: Karin Higgins/UC Davis)

They'd invited me to come talk with them about leadership in February 2009. On their way to their own careers, they'd wanted some advice about how to be an effective leader.

I'd surprised them with my mantra of "listen, listen, listen...bite your tongue...give others a chance to make your point."

I'm not sure there's a definable, teachable component to leadership. But I shared with them what I'd learned along the way through the academic and administrative ranks of professor, department head, biology programs executive officer, provost, executive vice chancellor and, ultimately, chancellor.

Residence hall meetings with undergrads provided opportunities for reciprocal learning. (Photo: Karin Higgins/UC Davis)

Here's what I believe makes for good leaders:

• **LISTENING.** Talking a lot may feel, to the speaker, like "leadership." But, believe me, it doesn't appear as leadership to the listener. Listening well does. And when you listen—truly listen—you might learn something you really need to know from the voice in the back of the room. Former Singaporean ambassador to the United Nations Tommy Ko—whom I'd met when traveling—encourages "deep listening," wisely observing that discovery starts with listening.

Listening well is especially important if you're new and you don't yet understand your organization's history and culture and where it was aiming to go before your arrival. What you learn will help inform your own vision of what's needed next.

• **CONVERSATION GUIDING.** If you have an important point to make, resist the temptation. You might know where your organization needs to go, but with a top-down deci-

Our Council of Deans and Vice Chancellors met informally for lunch each Tuesday—no agendas, just team-building, idea-exploring and information-sharing get-togethers. (Photo: Michael Brooks/The California Aggie)

Fall Convocation brought our campus family together at the beginning of each academic year to strengthen ties, share inspiring stories and energize one another to do our personal and collective best in the year ahead. (Photo: Karin Higgins/UC Davis)

sion you may lose the possible advantage of more discussion. And you'll lose the team that has to feel they've been a part of the decision if they're going to be great implementers.

Give others in the discussion a chance to make your point. If they do, tell them it was "a great point, an insightful, really wise point." Nudge it left or right a bit if it is not dead on.

If they don't make your point, you'll have to insert it into the conversation yourself. If at all possible, do it by building on or modifying someone else's point.

• **INCLUSIVENESS.** You have to be willing to bring into the conversation people you know will disagree with you, who will be contrary, who will have different views. If you can't respond sufficiently to their criticisms, maybe you have more thinking to do.

• **COURAGE.** When listening and conversation do not lead to consensus, take a seat in the lonely chair, think a while, perhaps sleep on it, and then make a decision. Float that decision by trusted advisers. Then make it, publicly, but make it with explanation: "These were the pros, these were the cons, and this is why I decided the way I did." You need to inspire confidence that you've given the matter adequate thought.

• **ACCOUNTABILITY.** Own your decision all the way through its implementation. Take responsibility for the way it turned out, even if you would have done things differently in carrying out that decision. What your team is saying and doing is part of the process you've approved and set into motion. Blaming others for things that may have gone wrong is not good leadership.

The deans and vice chancellors joined me at a bank of phones in the basement of Mrak Hall for a 1995 pilot project that invited people to dial in to ask questions, register concerns and simply connect with a senior administrator. Pictured with me here is former Letters and Science Dean Carol Tomlinson-Keasey. (Photo: Neil Michel/Axiom)

• **ACCESSIBILITY.** Invest time in understanding the interests and concerns of the many people who make up your organization. Drop by, invite conversations, develop relationships. Those connections will help you avoid pitfalls, help rescue you if you don't, and likely lead to lasting friendships.

• **CLEAR THINKING.** Do not over-respond to criticism. Do not over-respond to praise. Reality is somewhere in between.

• **DEVELOPING LEADERS.** Hire people who are better, who are smarter than you in their area.

Choose people who you believe will work well together. Deans, for example, have to be parochial—except when they are asked to deal as a team with campuswide issues. Then they have to rise above their parochial perspectives for the greater good of the university.

Let leaders lead. Let them make their own principle-based decisions. That's how leaders learn, and ultimately shine. They have to feel free to explore, to take wrong turns, to make mistakes. Making mistakes can be the best teacher. You—and they—will be most successful if, along the way, they feel that they've taught you a few things (which they undoubtedly will!).

Never, ever criticize them publicly. But, in one-on-one conversations, constructively address problems. The last thing you should want to do is take someone's confidence away. Praise them sincerely and often—with witnesses.

Pull them out of funks. People are often too hard on themselves.

• **FOSTERING A SENSE OF TEAM.** "Vision" is the easy part; you need a team to embrace it and to help implement it. One particularly effective vice chancellor (John Meyer) encouraged his people to recognize that their success wasn't complete until they'd helped their colleagues succeed. Teamwork—not competition—will most effectively help an organization achieve its goals.

• **TALKING STRAIGHT.** You've got to inspire confidence in your organization, and throughout it—especially through clearly rough patches. So be realistic in assessing the challenges, clear about how to address them, and optimistic about the organization's ability to not only survive but thrive once again.

• **KINDNESS.** A little bit goes a long, long way—and lifts your own spirits as well as the recipient's.

• **PERSONAL AMBITION.** Of course you have to have some, or you wouldn't be on the leadership path. But don't let it trump the good of the institution you're serving. That should always be paramount. The best leaders are most interested in ensuring their institution's people and accomplishments are recognized, not themselves.

• **INTEGRITY.** Without it? Game over.

A predecessor chancellor—Jim Meyer—instinctively understood how to draw the best out of his leadership team, embracing early on what became known as the Japanese style of management. UC Davis' chancellor from 1969 to 1987, he mentored by example and was clever enough that you usually thought his great idea was actually your own. More than anything else, he taught that consultation with all the university's constituencies was essential on most campus matters. The university benefited enormously from his vision and leadership.

UC Davis has proved an unusually fertile ground for administrators to hone their leadership skills, and for faculty to cut their teeth in administration. The list of those moving on to provost and president positions across the country is impressively long.

What those former UC Davis administrators received—and can perpetuate—is important: the opportunity to grow in a system that is collegial, values cooperation and encourages shared success. When leaders model that kind of behavior, it can't help but bring out the best in people. And what could be better for the institutions they serve?

James H. Meyer, UC Davis chancellor from 1969 to 1987, instinctively understood how to draw the best out of his leadership team. (Photo: UC Davis)

UC Davis-launched Leaders

These former UC Davis administrators went on to even greater leadership roles at other respected colleges and universities.

DAN ALDRICH: Acting chancellor, UC Santa Barbara, 1986-87; acting chancellor, UC Riverside, 1984-85; founding chancellor, UC Irvine, 1962-84; dean of agriculture for the University of California, 1958-62; department chair, UC Davis and UC Berkeley concurrently, 1955-58.

CAROL CARTWRIGHT: President, Bowling Green State University, 2008-11; president, Kent State University, 1991-2006; vice chancellor for academic affairs, UC Davis, 1988-91.

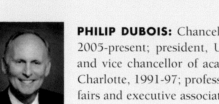

VERNON CHEADLE: Chancellor, UC Santa Barbara, 1962-77; professor and acting vice chancellor, UC Davis, 1950-62.

PHILIP DUBOIS: Chancellor, University of North Carolina, Charlotte, 2005-present; president, University of Wyoming, 1997-2005; provost and vice chancellor of academic affairs, University of North Carolina, Charlotte, 1991-97; professor, associate vice chancellor for academic affairs and executive associate dean of the College of Letters and Science, UC Davis, 1976-91.

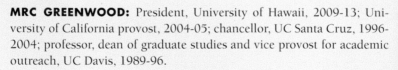

MRC GREENWOOD: President, University of Hawaii, 2009-13; University of California provost, 2004-05; chancellor, UC Santa Cruz, 1996-2004; professor, dean of graduate studies and vice provost for academic outreach, UC Davis, 1989-96.

ROBERT D. GREY: Interim provost, University of California, 2008-09; interim chancellor, UC Riverside, 2007-08; professor, assistant and associate dean of the College of Letters and Science, founding dean of the Division of Biological Sciences, and provost and executive vice chancellor, UC Davis, 1967-2001.

VIRGINIA HINSHAW: Chancellor, University of Hawaii at Manoa, 2007-12; provost and executive vice chancellor, UC Davis, 2001-07.

ELIZABETH LANGLAND: Vice provost and dean of the New College of Interdisciplinary Arts and Sciences, Arizona State University, 2007-13; provost and vice president for academic affairs, Purchase College/State University of New York, 2004-07; dean of the Division of Humanities, Arts and Cultural Studies, College of Letters and Science, UC Davis, 1999-2004.

DALE ROGERS MARSHALL: President, Wheaton College, 1992-2004; acting president and academic dean, Wellesley College, 1986-92; professor and associate dean of the College of Letters and Science and faculty assistant to the vice chancellor of academic affairs, UC Davis, 1972-86.

MARK MCNAMEE: Senior vice president and provost, Virginia Tech, 2001-present; dean, Division of Biological Sciences, UC Davis, 1993-2001; professor, UC Davis, 1975-2001.

ROBERT SHELTON: President, University of Arizona, 2006-11; executive vice chancellor and provost, University of North Carolina at Chapel Hill, 2001-06; vice provost for research, University of California, 1996-2001; vice chancellor for research, UC Davis, 1990-96; chair, Department of Physics, UC Davis, 1987-90.

CAROL TOMLINSON-KEASEY: Founding chancellor, UC Merced, 1998-2006; vice provost for academic initiatives, University of California, 1997-98; vice provost of faculty relations and of academic planning and personnel, and acting dean of the College of Letters and Science, UC Davis, 1992-97.

PHYLLIS WISE: Chancellor, University of Illinois at Urbana-Champaign, and vice president, University of Illinois, 2011-present; interim president, University of Washington, 2010-11; executive vice president and provost, University of Washington, 2005-10; dean of the Division of Biological Sciences, UC Davis, 2002-05.

FRED WOOD: Chancellor, University of Minnesota, Crookston, 2012-present; vice chancellor for student affairs (2007-12), interim vice provost for undergraduate studies (2004-07), College of Letters and Science associate dean (1991-2004), Department of Chemistry faculty member (1986-2012), UC Davis.

Wrestling with the Truth

The court finds the majority of [wrestling coach Michael] Burch's testimony wholly lacking in credibility.... Despite plaintiffs' belief to the contrary, Burch was not an ardent supporter of women's participation in intercollegiate competitive wrestling.[*]

—U.S. DISTRICT JUDGE FRANK C. DAMRELL, JR., IN HIS AUGUST 3, 2011, RULING IN A DISCRIMINATION LAWSUIT FILED BY THREE FORMER UC DAVIS WOMEN WRESTLERS

THE JUDGE CONFIRMED WHAT WE'D KNOWN ALL ALONG.

Former head wrestling coach Mike Burch—pitching for a full-time coaching position and then learning his part-time contract wouldn't be renewed—manipulated the trust of three young women wrestlers "for personal motives wholly unrelated to gender equity."[*]

Burch had told them that Associate Athletics Director Pam Gill-Fisher—not he—had cut them from his 30-slot wrestling roster after competitive tryouts, and that he'd been fired in retaliation for publicly defending their gender-discrimination complaint against the university (a complaint later dismissed by the U.S. Department of Education's Office for Civil Rights).

Preposterous charges, especially if you knew a whit about Pam.

U.S. District Judge Frank Damrell —the only judge to hear the entire

On May 29, 2001, UC Davis wrestlers protested what they believed to be the athletic department's removal of women from the team's roster. (Photo: Corey Yeaton/The California Aggie)

story, including lengthy witness testimony during a four-week bench trial the summer of 2011—simply didn't find Burch believable. "Indeed," he wrote, "the court finds that many of the underlying circumstances that gave rise to this litigation were a result of Burch's misrepresentations to plaintiffs."

---

[*]*This and all other quotations from Judge Damrell are taken from his Findings of Facts and Conclusions of Law issued at the conclusion of the trial in the case* Mansourian et al. v. Regents of the University of California et al., *(E.D. Cal.) 2:03-cv-2591 FCD EFB [Document 628, filed 8/3/11].*

Hallelujah! At last, an authoritative, definitive determination that Burch manipulated the students he was entrusted to lead.

Burch's blatant misrepresentations misled so many—from a sympathetic Assemblywoman (ill-advised by a former wrestler chief of staff) who threatened to withhold $44 million in construction funding for a campus science lab, to the American Association of University Women, which rallied to the young women's cause, providing nearly $100,000 for their lawsuit and a daily presence in the courtroom; California Sen. Dean Florez, who featured the women at a special Senate Select Committee hearing; and, most particularly, the young women themselves, who took Burch at his word and pursued an eight-year lawsuit whose discrimination claims were ultimately found groundless.

Contrary to their collective belief, Judge Damrell found that "the undisputed evidence demonstrates that Burch made virtually no efforts to establish a separate women's varsity team or even provide women wrestlers with adequate intercollegiate competitive opportunities until after such efforts could be personally beneficial to him."

Pam Gill-Fisher blazed a Title IX trail on campus and nationally, effectively advocating for greater opportunities for women athletes. (Photo: Jim von Rummelhoff/UC Davis)

A TRUE WOMEN'S CHAMPION

Most unforgivably, Burch's self-serving spin vilified Pam Gill-Fisher—a *true* champion of women.

Growing up on a farm, she worked right alongside her mother and father, oblivious to anyone's notion of gender roles—until Little League Baseball rejected her when she was 10 or 11. Until then, "I had never experienced being told I couldn't do something because I was female," she said at court.

Undaunted, Pam went on to excel as an athlete at Dixon High School and then competed as a five-sport Aggie athlete. All this before the 1972 landmark Title IX legislation prohibiting gender discrimination in federally funded educational institutions.

A national champion coach and a 28-year athletics administrator, she blazed a Title IX trail on campus and nationally. She helped build a program of athletic opportunities here that was unmatched by any university in the nation—leading *Sports Illustrated for Women* to twice name UC Davis the best NCAA Division II school for women athletes. And her efforts helped the campus produce three NCAA Woman of the Year award winners, an extraordinary national achievement.

A founding member of the National Association of Collegiate Women Athletics Administrators, Pam served as its president and on its board, was twice named its Division II Administrator of the Year and, in 2013, received its Lifetime Achievement Award.

From her earliest days at UC Davis, she effectively pushed for equal coaching and equitable benefits for women athletes—for such things as team-appropriate uniforms and equipment, athletic training, laundry services, participation and travel opportunities—and chaired multiple campus-initiated Title IX reviews. No more sewing matching shorts and gluing numbers on shirts for her volleyball team, no more scrounging stopwatches for the women's track and field team, no more player-purchased shoes for the women's basketball team, no more personal taping of women-athletes' ankles on a makeshift locker-room table. Not anymore. Pam was a true game-changer.

"I've worked my entire (nearly 30 year) career with Title IX stamped on my forehead," she said in June 2001 when Burch accused her of cutting the women from his wrestling roster. "I'm not about denying opportunity to women athletes."

A particularly revealing encounter between Pam and Burch in winter quarter 2000 is recounted in Judge Damrell's ruling: "Burch and Gill-Fisher discussed the prospects of Burch attaining full-time coaching status. Gill-Fisher explained that per UC Davis' gender equity plan, the next head coaches to go full-time would be from women's intercollegiate teams. In response, Burch suggested designating women's wrestling as a separate varsity team; Gill-Fisher pointed out that several other women's club sports were closer to meeting the requirements for an intercollegiate team. At the end of the meeting, Burch said he 'didn't give an F– about Title IX' before storming out and slamming the office door."

But Burch had convinced Lauren Mancuso, Arezou Mansourian and Christine Ng (who described him as her "hero" in court testimony) that he was their gender-equity champion, and that Pam and three other administrators—former Athletics Director Greg Warzecka, former Student Affairs Senior Associate Vice Chancellor Bob Franks and I—had treated them unfairly because of their gender, denying them the opportunity to participate in intercollegiate wrestling.

In truth, Pam was their true ally and potential mentor. She could have helped them expand their skills and develop more robust competition by establishing women's wrestling as a club sport and growing it to varsity status—a path rejected by the women (with Burch's encouragement) as a "demeaning demotion."

COURTROOM CONTENTION

So instead, we sat in opposition in the courtroom, with Lauren, Arezou and Christine on one side, flanked by family members and representatives of the AAUW (which, very disappointingly, counted Pam as a member yet invited only Burch and the three young women to address their local chapter). And we were on the other, supported by several UC Davis coaches and many of Pam's colleagues in the broader sports community—including her own mentor, Marya Welch, who pioneered women's athletics at UC Davis, guiding the program toward gender equity a full quarter-century before Title IX.

Also in the courtroom was another Title IX icon—revered expert witness Christine Grant, who, after a great deal of research on how we treated female student-athletes, appeared on our behalf, testifying for the first time ever *against* students in a Title IX case. And they were *our* students, misled by a coach they had trusted.

Their demand to be given a spot on the wrestling team regardless of their qualifications flew in the face of Title IX, Grant testified.

"I think to say that a young woman has a right to be on a particular team simply because she is a woman is giving that young woman preferential treatment," Grant testified. "And Title IX is not about preferential treatment; it is about equal opportunity."

COACHING STAFF

Mike Burch

Head Coach • 6th Year

In five years, Head Coach Mike Burch has moved the UC Davis wrestling program from a major rebuilding phase to a competitive Division I program. Burch's first efforts at UC Davis produced a nationally ranked Division I recruiting class. In the three years that followed, the Aggies collected 19 dual-meet wins in contrast to no wins during three previous years.

After his second season at UC Davis, Burch was named Men's Coach of the Year by the campus' student newspaper, *The California Aggie*.

In addition to the improved dual-meet record in 1998-99, Burch's Aggies had an unprecedented five placers at the Pacific-10 Championships, and another wrestler, David Yi, compete at the NCAA Division I Championships.

Last year, Burch brought the Pac-10 Championships to Recreation Hall. It marked the first time UC Davis hosted that conference's championship – in any sport.

Burch came to UC Davis from Brown University, where he was an assistant coach and graduate student from 1992-95. Prior to Brown, Burch was a graduate assistant at the University of Wisconsin, and an assistant coach at Diablo Valley College.

Raised in Redding, Burch was a high school state champion, and a fourth-place finisher at the Junior Nationals before attending Cal St. University, Bakersfield. As a freshman at Bakersfield, Burch was named to the NCAA Division I Freshman All-American team and was a four-year varsity starter on a team that won four consecutive Division II national titles.

In post-collegiate competition, Burch placed second in the Southeastern Regional Olympic Trials Qualifier in 1988, and second in the Western Regional Olympic Trials Qualifier in 1992.

Burch's graduate work is in ancient Mediterranean religions. He is also a University lecturer in the religion and exercise science departments.

10   2000-01 UC DAVIS WRESTLING

This 2000-01 UC Davis wrestling guide for news media was published in Mike Burch's last season as coach.

Judge Damrell agreed. He rejected Lauren's, Arezou's and Christine's claims that the university had eliminated a women's wrestling team or treated female wrestlers unfairly. And he dismissed their claims that Pam, Greg, Bob or I had discriminated against them based on their gender.

"Plaintiffs were not cut from the men's team because of their sex," the judge ruled. "Rather, plaintiffs were cut... because, like the other male student-athletes that did not make the roster, they could not compete at the Division I, Pac-10 level in intercollegiate men's wrestling."

Judge Damrell did find, however, that our overall athletics program fell short in meeting Title IX's "Prong 2" requirements while the three were enrolled, a time period that spanned 1998-2005. (Prong 2 calls for a history and practice of expanding women's intercollegiate athletic opportunities.)

He determined that we should have more quickly replaced lost opportunities for women athletes after we dropped two women's junior varsity teams in 2000-01 at the request of their coaches, who could no longer find

2000-01 AGGIES

Aggie Newcomers & Redshirts

Bryan Bacher
174 • Lebanon, Tenn.

Cris Brines
133 • Durham, Calif.

Cesar Correa
133 • Fairfield, Calif.

Flynn Ficker
285 • Potomac, Md.

Brett Hallenbeck
174 • Orinda, Calif.

John Kirkwood
174 • Rocklin, Calif.

Uno Kivi
197 • Reno, Nev.

Josh Ramirez
125 • Vista, Calif.

Ronnie Silva
197 • Clovis, Calif.

Steffan Weiner
184 • Fresno, Calif.

Stuart Young
165 • Leona Valley, Calif.

Women's Wrestling Club Program

For several years, UC Davis has had women participate in its program. Women's amateur wrestling is a new but rapidly growing sport in the U.S., with championships at the national and international levels.

At UC Davis, women's wrestling has an unofficial status, but women are encouraged to participate and develop their skills via the UC Davis Wrestling Club. The Aggie Open wrestling tournament includes a women's division and usually sees participation from women wrestlers throughout California.

This year's Aggie Open takes place Sunday, January 7, 2001 at Recreation Hall. The women's division at the Aggie Open is in its sixth year.

18   2000-01 UC DAVIS WRESTLING

The unofficial status of women's wrestling as a club program—not a varsity sport—is described above in this 2000-01 UC Davis wrestling guide for news media. The guide included a "Special thanks to Mike Burch" credit for its production.

sufficient intercollegiate-level competition for them. The coaches instead helped these JV athletes form club-sport teams so they could continue to play and improve their skills and potentially earn a spot on the varsity teams.

Title IX

Title IX, renamed the Patsy T. Mink Equal Opportunity in Education Act in honor of its principal author, was the first comprehensive federal law to prohibit sex discrimination in educational programs or activities, including intercollegiate athletics, at educational institutions receiving federal funds.

Part of the Education Amendments of 1972 to the Civil Rights Act of 1964, it reads: "No person in the United States shall, on the basis of sex, be excluded from participation in, be denied the benefits of, or be subjected to discrimination under any education program or activity receiving federal financial assistance."

Given the circumstance, we'd believed this was the right thing to do (and, notably, received no complaints at the time). And we'd believed our rate of replacement, in context, was reasonable—particularly given that we'd added three women's sports all at once in 1995-96 rather than spacing them out over time, increased funding for women's indoor track in 1999-2000 and added women's golf in 2005-06 (women's field hockey was subsequently added in 2009-10, though women's rowing, along with three men's sports, was eliminated later that year due to budget cuts). Today UC Davis sponsors 14 intercollegiate women's sports—compared to the Division I national average of 10.3—and nine men's sports.

Judge Damrell agreed the JV teams were eliminated for legitimate, nondiscriminatory reasons. But he concluded that, "despite its best intentions to the contrary, UC Davis did not have a continuing practice of program expansion at the time plaintiffs were students."

Even in his criticism, though, Judge Damrell recognized the campus's Title IX history and good-faith efforts and noted the complicating "dearth of guidance in this area of the law"—guidance missing since the law's 1972 passage straight through to Judge Damrell's 2011 ruling.

As the *Title IX Blog* noted in an Aug. 4, 2011, post by blog co-founder and Western New England College law professor Erin Buzuvis, an expert in gender and discrimination in sport, "...much of the court's decision is as pro-Davis as some of the headlines suggest. For one thing, even in its Title IX analysis, the court is careful to commend Davis for its history of program expansion, which included a rigorous self-analysis of compliance that resulted in the university's decision to add women's teams during a period of time in the 1980s when Title IX enforcement was lax and many other universities ignored the law."

What about the question of damages? Could the three young women demonstrate they'd suffered actual damages as a result of their Title IX claim?

Judge Damrell expressed serious doubt, noting the court "finds the evolution and potential impacts of this case troubling. It has been clear to the court throughout the arduous eight years of litigation that, for plaintiffs, this case has always been about wrestling.... The evidence at trial bore out that, while UC Davis failed to comply with Title IX during the time that plaintiffs were students at UC Davis, plaintiffs' complaints about defendants' conduct relating to wrestling were meritless. This troubling juxtaposition of the court's conclusions would seem to place severe limitations on the damages these plaintiffs recover."

We ended up settling to avoid yet more costly time in court. The university agreed to pay $1.35 million to the three young women's counsel for attorneys' fees and costs incurred during this years-long case—likely significantly less than what may have been ordered if the issue had been decided by a jury. Nothing was paid to Lauren, Arezou and Christine.

We'd earlier settled with Burch, as well—a 2007 decision to pay $725,000 that still rankles though I know it was the prudent thing to do. Burch had solicited and won what Judge Damrell later described as ill-informed "interference and advocacy by media and public figures," and who's to say he couldn't similarly sway a jury? And he was seeking punitive damages, as well. The university's financial exposure was just too great.

LESSONS LEARNED

So were there lessons learned over more than eight years of litigation and public acrimony?

Dot every "i" and cross every "t"—a takeaway voiced by one of Pam's community college administrator courtroom colleagues hoping to learn from our experience.

Document a personnel decision *when it's made*—especially if you intend to wait (as Human Resources customarily advises to avoid lame-duck conduct) until 30 days before the appointment's end to inform an employee. Waiting—without documenting an earlier decision date—will make it all the harder to refute a later retaliation claim, proving just how costly not having a paper record can be.

> *An exemplary reputation, honestly won, can be outmatched by a campaign of misinformation capitalizing on public misimpressions.*

And understand that an exemplary reputation, honestly won, can be outmatched by a campaign of misinformation capitalizing on public misimpressions.

While our legal case is now closed, it will likely be a while before UC Davis recovers in the court of public opinion.

For Pam, that day has already come with the father of one of our three former students. Standing next to her in the courthouse cafeteria line, he shared: "If we knew then what we know now, we wouldn't be here."

Seeing the Invisible Disability

What will come next? Will we need to give extra time on exams to stupid people?
—A UC DAVIS DEAN, 1986

IN 1985, ON THE EVE OF HIS GRADUATION, AN UNDERGRADUATE VENTURED to the Chancellor's Office to share a concern.

He had dyslexia, he confided to me and Jerry Hallee, assistant to the executive vice chancellor. And, despite his coping skills, earning a UC Davis degree hadn't been easy for him because of this information-processing disorder.

He didn't want it to be as challenging for those learning-disabled students who would follow him.

It wasn't a matter of intellectual ability, he conveyed, but of having to learn differently.

"We're not slow—we're just *slow*," I remember this young man saying with a smile.

He hoped that Jerry and I would consider adding services for students with learning disabilities to those the campus already provided for students with more obvious needs—for example, those who were blind or deaf or depended on wheelchairs to get around.

In the mid-1980s, what he was proposing was quite unusual. And yet, there he was, just 21 or 22 years old, making a case for others when he was ready to move on to the next chapter in his life.

He may never fully know what his advocacy set into motion—or how grateful I am that he thought just maybe he could make a difference.

(Illustration: Scott Ahrens/ UC Davis Magazine)

He convinced Jerry and me that the campus needed to learn more and do more to address these students' needs.

Jerry's own son had been diagnosed with dyslexia in elementary school. So he under-

Jerry Hallee and I scoured the 1985 student yearbook and commencement programs, hoping to recognize the face or the name of our unsung undergraduate hero. (Photo: Karin Higgins/UC Davis)

stood that appropriate support could make all the difference in the world. But much *wasn't* understood about learning disabilities in the 1980s. For instance, people generally thought that if you were diagnosed in elementary school and had gotten some accommodations there and perhaps in high school, you would outgrow your learning disability by the time you got to college. This particular kind of disability was also incorrectly thought to be a developmental issue, not hard wiring. So it was unusual then for colleges to even think about providing special services.

To further complicate the matter, clusters of these high-achieving kids were flying under the radar in both elementary and high school and were never diagnosed. Through tenacity and giftedness, they made it into a competitive four-year university but then ran into trouble with the tougher curriculum, the increased workload and the quicker-paced quarter system. They often didn't even realize they were learning disabled; they just knew they had to work harder and longer than their peers.

Many were intellectually gifted and extremely articulate, yet couldn't read or write well; some also had trouble with math; and all were slower than molasses taking exams. That didn't help win the empathy of college faculty, who generally equated not processing information very quickly with not being very intelligent.

The dean who asked in 1986 if we'd next need to give extra exam time to stupid people wasn't alone in his skepticism. Faculty at his lunch table that day had expressed the same doubt about such "invisible" disabilities that couldn't be readily verified. How could they judge if the need was real and not simply an attempt to get extra help that wasn't deserved? And what kinds of accommodations could faculty reasonably be expected to make?

These were big questions. And they were understandable ones, given what was known then and given the lack of a clear road map for colleges and universities that were just beginning to see a surge in students with learning disabilities.

At that point, most of the research and intervention had focused on learning-disabled children rather than on adult learners. Most learning-disabled adults—likely including members of our own faculty and staff—had never been diagnosed. So faculty generally weren't familiar with this form of disability in their students. And those who were themselves learning-disabled but had toughed it out without special help may have believed that, if they could do it, so could their students.

But our dyslexic graduating student had convinced me we needed to re-examine our assumptions and consider new possibilities.

Soon after his visit, Jerry and I pulled together leaders in our Student Affairs and Academic Affairs offices (principally Tom Dutton, Bob Cello, Bob Chason, Yvonne Marsh and Maureen Brodie) for several meetings. They agreed that we needed to explore appropriate accommodations for these newly identified students, and to more broadly interpret the 1978 federal disability regulations that focused heavily on students with visible physical disabilities.

That fall, in 1985, I appointed two task forces. The first, headed by Professor of Psychiatry Margaret ("Marge") Steward, was to determine a credible method for identifying and testing learning-disabled students. The second, headed by Professor of Education Carl Spring, was to recommend appropriate accommodations and services for these students.

Both task forces finished their work by the end of spring quarter 1986, and each supported the hiring of a learning disabilities specialist.

The Steward task force confirmed the relatively recent availability of rigorous diagnostic processes to reliably identify learning-disabled students. It recommended that a to-be-hired learning disabilities specialist review a student's learning history, gather existing documentation, and refer the student for a current assessment if needed. It also identified several campus offices capable of performing an assessment; ultimately, the UC Davis Department of Education agreed to do the testing at a reduced cost to referred students. The task force also identified a critical need to educate the campus about learning-disabled students, noting in particular that "faculty and academic deans should be an early and continuing educational target."

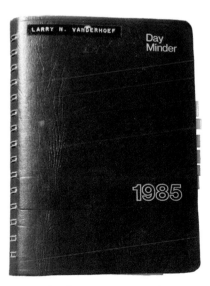

The Spring task force recommended a reduced courseload and/or waiving of the minimum progress requirement for certified learning-disabled students—a waiver of the quantitative, not qualitative, standard of scholarship. It also recommended that faculty give additional time for examinations or alternative exam formats for certified learning-disabled students; while "regular" students might also benefit from added time, it said, "scores of LD students would be improved significantly, while scores of regular students would be improved

A search of my 1985 appointment book yielded no clues to the identity of the undergraduate who unexpectedly dropped by. (Photo: Karin Higgins/UC Davis)

only marginally." And it recommended an exemption from the 12-unit foreign language requirement, noting that "learning a foreign language is uniquely difficult, if not an exercise in futility, for many LD students."

The task force also advocated for a learning disability specialist who would counsel students and assist them in interacting with faculty or campus committees, and recommended such services as one-to-one tutoring and learning skills workshops as well as priority access to taped textbooks and to Computer Center personal computers with an easy-to-learn word-processor and spell-checker.

With the task force reports in hand, we next sought the blessing of the Academic Senate that fall. Then-Senate Chair Dick Gable couldn't have been a better partner.

In 1986-87, 47 students requested assistance for a learning disability—up from 11 in 1985-86. In 2014-15, more than 400 students asked for this support.

"Dick made just an enormous difference," recalled Marge Steward. "He was very receptive to the arguments we made and the clinical stories we told him and the research we presented. He helped change the structural requirements for graduation in a way that made sense for these kids."

In spring 1987, the Senate's Representative Assembly approved two of the three major recommendations—reducing courseload and/or waiving the minimum progress requirement, and providing added exam time or alternate exam formats for learning-disabled students. The third—waiving the foreign-language requirement—was left to the College of Letters and Science. The college's Executive Committee preferred to issue waivers on a case-by-case basis, prompting this response from Dick Gable to Larry Peterman, chair of the L&S faculty:

"I can understand why the Executive Committee wishes to be careful about granting blanket exemptions. However, I do not agree that the category of learning disabled students is 'very broad.' The procedure for identification is precise and rigorous, both as to the steps to be taken and the persons to be involved in certifying students who have learning disabilities….

"Nonetheless, your decision has been made. Therefore, I want to inquire about the procedure for granting exemptions on a case-by-case basis…. A clear statement of these criteria would be helpful to the persons involved in certifying those who have learning disabilities."

L&S' response, with its history of case-by-case exemption request approvals, led Dick to conclude that we'd be able to accommodate the needs of students with learning disabilities.

So, with the last hurdle hurdled, I provided funding to hire a learning disabilities specialist—a position first and currently held by Christine O'Dell, an exceptionally insightful and dedicated professional. In her first report, Chris noted that, in 1986-87, 47 students had requested assistance for a learning disability—up from 11 in 1985-86. In 2014-15, more than 400 students asked for this support.

That help is life-altering, attest two alumni who benefited early on from the advocacy of our 1985 graduating dyslexic student.

"In short, the [Student Disability Center] changed my life," says Christopher Ott, a 1996 civil engineering graduate. With the center's help, he was able to guide fellow dyslexic engineering students and to teach coping strategies to other learning-disabled students at a private Davis learning center. Christopher is currently CEO of an engineering company specializing in water-treatment clean technologies and has several patented systems in use for sustainable farming in Europe and the United States.

Abigail Tilden, who graduated in 1994 with a degree in rhetoric and communication and a minor in education, adds, "There is no doubt that without the help and guidance I received from the Student Disability Center I would not have succeeded personally, academically or professionally." Abigail came to UC Davis as an undiag-

Located in the Cowell Building, the Student Disability Center is staffed by disability professionals who specialize in different areas of disability—learning, vision, hearing, medical, psychological and mobility. (Photo: Gregory Urquiaga/UC Davis)

nosed transfer student who, despite heroic effort, soon found herself on academic probation. Nudged by a friend, she finally sought help, beginning "a process of exploration that would take me from near academic extinction to successful mastery"—despite an additional diagnosis of Attention Deficit Hyperactivity Disorder. She went on to earn a master's degree in education and to become a disability specialist first at UC Berkeley and then at UC Davis.

I wish I could share these stories, and so many others just like them, with our 1985 undergraduate hero. I can still picture him—tall, maybe 6'2"; dark hair; medium build. But I can't recall his name. After so many years, memories have dimmed and old appointment calendars haven't been helpful. After several fruitless efforts, I've finally made peace with the notion that I'll likely never be able to thank him properly.

Marge Steward calls him our unknown soldier. "He started the ball rolling, and all kinds of people in all kinds of corners of the university have picked it up and run with it."

He's made an enormous difference. I hope he somehow knows that.

16 College Park

I will never, ever forgive the university . . . .
—DEAN EMERITUS KNOWLES RYERSON, FIRST OCCUPANT OF THE
    UC DAVIS CHANCELLOR'S RESIDENCE

SIXTEEN COLLEGE PARK, A PLUM PIECE OF PROPERTY IN DAVIS' HISTORIC
College Park neighborhood, is an address with a past—and a bit of a checkered one, at that.

Since 1937, it's been home to each of UC Davis' chancellors and, in the campus's early days, to its chief administrator, Knowles Ryerson.

It was Knowles who built the original 16 College Park residence, a quaint, small Cape Cod in a foliage-sparse neighborhood of barley flats.

Entitled to a university-provided house, Knowles said no, explaining in his memoirs, "We've planned our own home and I want

The UC Davis Chancellor's Residence at 16 College Park. (Photo: Gregory Urquiaga/UC Davis)

to feel that if I want to throw a brick through the front window of the living room, I can do it without calling up and getting the business office's permission."

That good-humored response was vintage Knowles, whom Rosalie and I got to know when we first came to UC Davis in 1984. We met with him three or four times, just for the purpose of enjoyable long conversations and the better sense of campus history that they gave us.

Knowles had fond recollections of the house and the grounds. His personal home, it didn't possess features that argued for its being the Chancellor's Residence, except for the wonderful back yard, a very deep, double-wide lot—a great place for outdoor receptions and dinners.

He put that back yard to particularly good use just after World War II, spending his own money to build a sheltered brick barbecue for returning GIs and their families to use. On the back wall, he affixed a 7-by-12-foot army map so the returning soldiers could point out to their girlfriends or wives where they'd served.

Knowles and his wife, Emma, added a set of dishes and all the needed barbecue equipment. "Then we said to the GIs, 'Now here are the keys; it's all out there, even a supply of wood. Have yourself a time!.... The noise won't bother us—we'll be glad to hear you back there.'"

And so, for some 15 years, the Ryersons warmly welcomed students, faculty, staff and other visitors to their home. With their example, the "Davis Spirit" was firmly taking root—that defining sense of caring, encouraging and friendliness that I've always believed uniquely characterizes our UC Davis family. Knowles is credited as that spirit's early source and strength.

Knowles Ryerson, the Davis campus's first leader. (Photo: UC Davis)

Unfortunately, that caring wasn't reciprocated by the University of California when Knowles learned Stanley Freeborn was to replace him as UC Davis' first provost—and that the Ryerson residence was expected to be part of Freeborn's appointment package, effective July 1, 1952.

Immediately adjacent to the campus and within walking and biking distance, the 16 College Park home was ideal for Freeborn. "We were under constant pressure to get out of the house as Stan wanted to move in even though we hadn't yet decided to sell," Knowles recounted.

The Regents' secretary and treasurer, Bob Underhill, pressed him and personally negotiated the sale. Described as an unrelenting, vigorous negotiator, he dictated appraisal terms unacceptable to Knowles. "No, this is an appraisal, not a condemnation," Knowles responded. "I still reserve the right of refusal."

Ultimately, the university prevailed, paying a minimal amount for the property. Knowles had been sold down the river, according to a faculty member who heard Underhill announce the offer to the Regents.

Many years later, those wounds still hadn't healed. Though disappointed to be passed over for Provost in 1952 and for Chancellor in 1958, Knowles told me he fully understood that ultimately the appointment decision was the university's to make.

"But I will never, ever forgive the university for taking away my home."

Before turning over the keys, he salvaged from the roof a special weather vane equipped with a telescope. Made to order for him by the house's architect, Edgar Mayberry of Pasadena, it followed him to the Bay Area. "I said [to the university], 'That doesn't go with the house; that's mine.'"

Knowles departed Davis for Berkeley in 1952, becoming dean of UC Berkeley's College of

Agriculture. And he moved to a beautiful little home in Kensington, overlooking San Francisco and the Bay. It was there that he lived out his life until he died in 1990, at the age of 97.

SMALL HOUSE, BIG EXPECTATIONS

The Ryerson home at 16 College Park subsequently served as the official residence of several UC Davis leaders—Provost/Chancellor Stanley Freeborn and Chancellors Emil Mrak, Jim Meyer and Ted Hullar.

On the eve of Jim Meyer's appointment in 1969, the UC Regents could see that Jim's five kids would stretch the little bungalow's capacity. So they authorized a $19,000 addition—a little cottage to be built out back.

In 1987, Jim passed the keys to his successor, Ted Hullar. After Ted and Joan moved out in February 1994, the nearly 60-year-old house lay vacant, its foundation crumbling, its electrical system failing, its moss-damaged roof deteriorating, and its steep stairwells no longer up to code. Dry rot and termite damage had also taken a toll, and asbestos and lead were detected throughout. As well, the house just wasn't laid out well for the events a chancellor must host. In particular, I remember a reception where Ted posted himself on the border of two rooms, leaning in to one and then the other as he made remarks, and I recall a dinner where a couple dozen people were divided among three rooms—not a lot of crosstalk that evening or on so many other occasions.

But the campus community soon came to the rescue. In 1995, a committee of faculty, staff, student, alumni, donor and community representatives recommended the house

The original Chancellor's Residence at 16 College Park. (Photo: Todd Hammond/The Davis Enterprise)

be demolished and reconstructed, with the $1.26 million in costs covered by non-state funds from the UC Office of the President (after a little coaxing from Regent Roy Brophy, who knew OP had given funding for renovations of the UC Berkeley Chancellor's Residence) and from private funds raised by the campus's Ryerson Society. Private dollars also covered the $134,000 cost of site development and the $185,000 cost of furnishings for the public portion of the 7,779-square-foot house.

The committee believed 16 College Park was an essential campus asset—much more than simply the personal residence of whoever happened to be UC Davis' chancellor.

It uniquely represented and fostered the Davis campus tradition of community, and enabled the chancellor to effectively fulfill a growing public role.

"It isn't the same experience to attend an event that takes place in a campus facility, however functional and pleasant it may be," committee chair Janet Hamilton, vice chancellor for administration, noted at the time. "Nothing substitutes for the feeling of intimacy and privilege that accompanies a personal invitation to the Chancellor's home…. For many, the visits to this house are included in their fondest memories of the Davis campus experience."

So with the committee's endorsement and the commitment of non-state and gift funds, the work began.

STARTING OVER—BUT WITH CARE FOR KEEPSAKE TREES

It took just 90 minutes for the original residence to be razed on June 10, 1996, but not before two hummingbird hatchlings nesting in a trellised walkway could be rushed by Avian Science's Alida Morzenti to a Santa Rosa woman expert in hand-feeding baby birds. The residence's backyard cottage was also rescued—purchased by a College Park neighbor, then hoisted up and wheeled a block away to its new home.

We looked to San Francisco architectural firm William Turnbull Associates for a simple but elegant design that met our three criteria—the new house must be versatile and functional for university events, it must take advantage of the property's natural beauty, and it must not overpower the other homes in the neighborhood. Turnbull delivered a beautiful design that featured a courtyard ringed by a combination of private and public spaces that met the needs of both a residence and a public venue.

The original residence was razed in June 1996. (Photo: Neil Michel/Axiom)

Ridge Builders Group of Davis constructed the home throughout 1997, taking pains to work very carefully around the property's old trees, guided by on-site supervisor and UC Davis alum David Kane. The reward was an arboreal "peacefulness to the courtyard" that Ridge Builders Group co-owner and UC Davis alum Bob Schneider said he found especially satisfying.

The home's exceptional grounds were indeed well worth preserving. They were designed and planted by Knowles, an internationally known horticulturalist and plant biologist who served for a time as chief of the U.S. Department of Agriculture's Bureau of Plant Industry.

Robert Munyon, 1940 student body president, who helped plant the two Modesto ashes in the Chancellor's Residence backyard. (Photo: UC Davis)

"I planted everything that's there," he said. Especially striking are a "heritage" Himalayan spruce among several sycamores in the front yard and one particularly statuesque Chinese wingnut and two Modesto ashes in the back yard.

He had a little help with the ashes, though, as 1940 student body president Robert Munyon told the story. Just elected to office, he'd gotten a call from Knowles, who asked him to come by the house. Certain that they would sit down and lay out the campus's future, he came running.

"Well, we did talk a bit about my recent election as student body president, but we very quickly got around to another topic," Bob told me several years ago at an event in the residence's back yard. "Dr. Ryerson had recently injured his back and he wasn't able to lift heavy things or even navigate very easily. So he asked me for a favor, taking me to the back yard where the two ashes were waiting to be planted, and showed me where the holes should be dug. After a few hours of very labor-intensive work on my part, we got the two trees in the ground. And that was the beginning of these two beautiful trees."

I remember on many a hot day being grateful for those trees, by now nearly 70 feet tall, because they gave shade to over half of the back yard. Our cat, Luke, spent one of his nine lives when he fell from the highest reaches of one of the ashes, hit the ground with a thump heard by residence manager Jill Woodard, and knocked himself out. To Jill's immense relief (they were fast friends), a minute later he got up and wobbled off, and never showed any signs of injury.

The back yard's Chinese wingnut also has a tale. Knowles planted it from seed shortly after he returned from one of his trips to Asia. Curious to see what would sprout, he brought a few seeds back for the national arboretum along with a seedling for his new back yard. A few decades ago, the tree was discovered to be an excellent root-stock source for commercial walnut trees. Word got around that we had one of just a few in the area, so walnut farmers would occasionally show up at the house, hoping to be able to gather some seeds.

Over the years, the residence has had many memorable visitors—from Chilean President Michelle Bachelet to Secretary of State Henry Kissinger, Bishop Desmond Tutu, California Gov. Arnold Schwarzenegger, physicist Stephen Hawking, historian Doris Kearns Goodwin, novelist Salman Rushdie, newsman Mike Wallace, vintner philanthropists Robert and Margrit Mondavi, and cartoonist Garry Trudeau (an over-night guest whose midnight rustling in the residence's kitchen rousted Rosalie for a bowl-of-cereal chat about caring for aging parents).

But I know Rosalie recalls most fondly the many, many students, staff and faculty who were so honored to be invited to the Chancellor's Residence that they took home the menu card or didn't want to relinquish their name tags at the event's end.

I particularly enjoyed our backyard Picnic Day ice cream socials—especially watching the kids messily make ice cream sundaes. When they'd licked their last spoonful, I told them that now they had to get right back in line for a second helping. I still smile thinking about *Davis Enterprise* columnist Bob Dunning's daughter Maev, who admitted to me: "This is already my third!"

TRULY THE UC DAVIS FAMILY'S HOME

Though Rosalie and I have owned a house in Davis since our 1984 arrival from Maryland, we appreciated our 11 years at 16 College Park. We always knew it was not our home, but the university's—entrusted to us as a uniquely special venue for hosting members of our extended campus family and for conducting university business.

We emptied our personal home in late December 1997 to fill the 2,859-square-foot private part of the residence—a family room, master bedroom, three additional bedrooms, three bathrooms, laundry, catering kitchen and breakfast nook. The university furnished the 4,920-foot public portion of the residence, which includes a large living room and entry, a formal dining room that seats up to 12 guests (campus arts benefactor Barbara Jackson, expert with a needle, fashioned a special tablecloth for the room's elegantly substantial table), a large "gallery" room that accommodates up to 50 seated guests, a catering staging area and pantry, a wine cellar, a study, a guest suite with sitting room and bedroom, restrooms, a manager's office and a two-car garage.

> *We always knew it was not our home, but the university's—entrusted to us as a uniquely special venue for hosting members of our extended campus family and for conducting university business.*

I realize that times and circumstances (and chancellors' needs) change. The house's public/private demarcations have become less clear, with personal furnishings now throughout the residence and the university's furniture (initially put into storage) now dispersed.

The tree-shaded Chancellor's Residence courtyard can accommodate sit-down meals for 250 and receptions for more than 500. A smaller garden area beyond the breezeway is ideal for smaller receptions. (Photo: UC Davis)

I hope this doesn't signal a change in the house's use, that the UC Davis Chancellor's Residence will continue to be broadly open to our campus family and our community for decades to come.

As Knowles Ryerson recognized from the very beginning, 16 College Park has a special power to perpetuate the defining "Davis Spirit."

More than 75 years later, I believe that's a legacy still worthy of embracing.

Epilogue

The best-laid plans of mice and men often go awry.
—ADAPTED FROM "TO A MOUSE" BY POET ROBERT BURNS

Midway through the writing of this book, the unthinkable happened.

I suffered a stroke (caused when a vessel in the brain ruptures or is blocked by a clot).

But for some 15 hours I failed to recognize its signs, to accept that it could really be happening. Not a stroke. Not me.

It'd started about 3 p.m. Friday, Nov. 30, 2012. I'd suddenly felt ill and closed the door between my office and my assistant Cindy Contreras' office. My vision had blurred and I'd felt that the world was zipping by me as if I were on a carnival ride. And I was losing my sense of balance.

Something had surely gone wrong, but I felt that if I got home and rested it would get better. In hindsight, that was silly thinking, but I had not been sick in 23 years.

I didn't share with Cindy, or with anyone else, the symptoms I was experiencing. I simply told her that I wasn't feeling well and was going home. I walked out the back door of the Conference Center to the parking lot and managed to drive home, stopping my car a few times along the way to calm my spinning vision.

At home, I fell asleep on the bed but each time I awoke I was less able to navigate. Rosalie wanted me to go straightaway to Sutter Davis Hospital's Emergency Room, just 10 minutes away, but I refused. We finally compromised: If I wasn't better by 6 a.m.—15 hours after the first symptoms—she could call an ambulance. So, at 6 a.m., the ambulance and two other red-lights-flashing emergency vehicles arrived. I was conscious but unable to walk or do much of anything with the right side of my body. And still I was convinced it was going to be a quick fix.

The ER docs set me straight, and so began my intense "course" on stroke biology—including some six weeks total as an in-patient at our UC Davis Medical Center in Sacramento.

I wish I hadn't needed to belatedly learn this lesson. I wish I'd better known how to recognize and respond to the signs of a stroke—the No. 4 cause of death in the United States (one death every four minutes) and the No. 1 cause of preventable disability worldwide.

The American Heart Association and American Stroke Association remind us all that a stroke is largely preventable, treatable and beatable.

We can be prepared by learning and sharing the F.A.S.T. acronym—Facial drooping, Arm weakness, Speech difficulty and Time to call 9-1-1—and responding quickly. Ischemic stroke patients should receive treatment within the first 3-4 hours. As my own physician counsels, "Time is brain." Rapid, early treatment can prevent long-term damage and offers the best chance of recovery.

You can reduce your risk for stroke by managing your blood pressure, eating better, getting physically active, losing excess weight, lowering your cholesterol, reducing your blood sugar and not smoking, the American Stroke Association advises.

I learned all this the hard way. I hope you won't.

I've made enormous strides since the first frightening days of hospitalization when I could barely wiggle a finger on my right side and pondered how I could ever adjust to such a compromised state of living. Amazingly, the brain can rewire and skills can be relearned.

I've rebounded significantly—"I'm upright!" I'll respond with a smile when people see me about and ask how I'm doing. Now in my 70s, I know I'm also experiencing the inevitable effects of aging (names don't come as quickly as they once did, and a cane now comes in handy when I'm tired or walking in the wind). As a scientist, I'm frustrated that I can't cleanly separate stroke impacts from aging impacts. But I'm adjusting, and I'm doing well. I work at my office desk every day; serve on multiple university and regional boards; attend numerous Mondavi Center, B Street Theatre, Sacramento Ballet, and music and dance department performances; support our football and men's and women's basketball teams at most every game; enjoy U.S. and international travels with Rosalie; and work out three to four days a week at the ARC.

If only I could reprise my "Exercise Seminar" squash games with my good friend Charley Hess…then I'd feel my recovery was complete. I'm realistic enough to know that that's probably not in the cards.

But, even so, I know I'm awfully lucky. I survived.

Postscript:

Well, the unthinkable happened again.

Another stroke—this time on Nov. 2, 2014. It had all the hallmarks of the first one, but in spades.

So I'm traveling that recovery road one more time. But I did it before and I know I can do it again. Just watch me!

THINK YOU ARE HAVING A STROKE? CALL 9-1-1 IMMEDIATELY!

F.A.S.T. is an easy way to remember the sudden signs of stroke. When you can spot the signs, you'll know that you need to call 9-1-1 for help right away. **F.A.S.T.** is:

FACE DROOPING—Does one side of the face droop or is it numb? Ask the person to smile. Is the person's smile uneven?

ARM WEAKNESS—Is one arm weak or numb? Ask the person to raise both arms. Does one arm drift downward?

SPEECH DIFFICULTY—Is speech slurred? Is the person unable to speak or hard to understand? Ask the person to repeat a simple sentence, like "The sky is blue." Is the sentence repeated correctly?

TIME TO CALL 9-1-1—If someone shows any of these symptoms, even if the symptoms go away, call 9-1-1 and get the person to the hospital immediately. Check the time so you'll know when the first symptoms appeared.

Source: American Heart Association, Inc.

SAMPLING OF RESOURCES REVIEWED

American Stroke Association, *Stroke Warning Signs and Symptoms* (http://www.strokeassociation.org/STROKEORG/).

Richard C. Atkinson, *The Pursuit of Knowledge: Speeches and Papers of Richard C. Atkinson*; edited by Patricia A. Pelfrey with a foreword by David S. Saxon (Berkeley and Los Angeles, CA: University of California Press, 2007).

Roy Brophy, "Regents made a mistake on affirmative action" (opinion column, *The Sacramento Bee*, Nov. 9, 1995).

Erin E. Buzuvis, "District Court Reaches Decision in UC Davis Title IX Case" (*Title IX Blog*, Aug. 4, 2011).

Sammy Caiola, *The Sacramento Bee*, "Burn Doctor Helps Kids Heal, Thrive," Aug. 28, 2014.

The Carnegie Foundation for the Advancement of Teaching, *Campus Life: In Search of Community* (San Francisco, CA: Jossey-Bass, May 1990).

U.S. District Judge Frank C. Damrell, Jr., *Mansourian et al. v. Regents of the University of California et al.*, (E.D. Cal.) 2:03-cv-2591 FCD EFB, Memorandum and Order Setting Forth Findings of Fact and Conclusions of Law [Document 628, filed Aug. 3, 2011].

Erik Dane and Michael G. Pratt, *Exploring Intuition and Its Role in Managerial Decision Making*, (Academy of Management Review, 2007, Vol. 32, No. 1, pp. 33-54).

Richard Davis, *Justices and Journalists: The U.S. Supreme Court and the Media* (Cambridge, UK: Cambridge University Press, 2011).

James J. Duderstadt, *The View from the Helm: Leading the American University during an Era of Change* (Ann Arbor, MI: The University of Michigan Press, 2010, 2009, 2008, 2007).

Cristina Gonzalez, *Clark Kerr's University of California: Leadership, Diversity and Planning in Higher Education* (New Brunswick, N.J.: Transaction Publishers, 2011).

Allie Grasgreen, "Criticism of athletics spending in wake of Penn State unlikely to slow growth" (*Inside Higher Ed*, July 23, 2012).

Dave Jones, "Vanderhoef addresses compensation criticism" (*Dateline UC Davis*, Feb. 3, 2006).

Dave Jones, "Higher education talent pool at UC Davis" (*Dateline UC Davis*, July 20, 2007).

Dave Jones, "Senate questions recruitment process" (*Dateline UC Davis*, April 17, 2008).

Knight Commission On Intercollegiate Athletics, *Restoring the Balance: Dollars, Values, and the Future of College Sports* (multimedia report available at restoringbalance.knightcommission.org, 2010).

Nicholas D. Kristof, "Not So Crazy in Tehran," "In Iran, They Want Fun, Fun, Fun," "Pinched and Griping in Iran," "Hugs from Iran" (*The New York Times*, June 23, 2012, June 20, 2012, June 16, 2012, June 13, 2012).

Doug Lederman, Kevin Kiley and Scott Jaschik, "Concerns About Sports, Backing for Obama: a Survey of Presidents" (*Inside Higher Ed*, March 8, 2012).

Adam Liptak, "Court Backs Michigan on Affirmative Action" (*The New York Times*, April 22, 2014).

James H. Meyer Oral History Project: Oral History Interview with James H. Meyer, Feb. 5, 7, 10, 21 and 24, 1992; interviews conducted by Susan E. Douglass (Sacramento, CA: Oral History Program, California State University, 1992).

Emil M. Mrak – A Journey Through Three Epochs: Food Prophet, Creative Chancellor, Senior Statesman of Science, Volumes I and II; interviews conducted by A. I. Dickman (Davis, CA: Regents of the University of California, 1974).

Janet Napolitano, "How to diversify a campus, in spite of the Supreme Court" (*The Washington Post*, April 25, 2014).

The National Collegiate Athletic Association, "*Revenues & Expenses, 2004-2012, NCAA Division I Intercollegiate Athletics Programs Report*" (Indianapolis, IN: April 2012).

The NCAA News, "Musical Chairs," October 11, 2004.

The New York Times, "Racial Equality Loses at the Court" editorial, April 22, 2014.

Oral history interview with James H. Meyer, October 25, 1995, by Lorena Herrig; 53-minute videocassette (Davis, CA: UC Davis Emeriti Association, 1995).

Patricia A. Pelfrey, *Entrepreneurial President: Richard Atkinson and the University of California, 1995-2003* (Berkeley and Los Angeles, CA: University of California Press, 2012).

James Richardson, "Political axing of affirmative action galls UC's Brophy" (*The Sacramento Bee*, July 29, 1995).

James Richardson, "UC kills affirmative action: Wilson triumphs at rowdy meeting" (*The Sacramento Bee*, July 21, 1995).

James Richardson, "Wilson muscle tied to UC vote" (*The Sacramento Bee*, July 22, 1995).

William Rodarmor, "Affirmative Reaction" (*California Monthly*, April 1995).

William Rodarmor, "A Delicate Balance: The Arts at Cal" (*California Monthly*, December 1995).

Knowles A. Ryerson, *The World Is My Campus* by Knowles A. Ryerson; introduction by John W. Oswald; interviews conducted by Joann L. Larkey (Davis, CA: Regents of the University of California, 1977).

The Sacramento Bee, "UC: The politics came first" editorial, July 22, 1995.

Ann F. Scheuring, *Abundant Harvest: The History of the University of California, Davis*; foreword by California State Librarian Kevin Starr (Davis, CA: Regents of the University of California, 2001).

Ann Foley Scheuring, *Doctors and Scholars: Celebrating 25 Years of Excellence at the University of California, Davis, School of Medicine; An Anniversary History* (Davis, CA: Regents of the University of California, 1996).

Murray A. Sperber, "Five myths about college sports" (*The Washington Post*, March 13, 2015).

UC Davis NewsWatch video reports (Center for the Arts campaign launch and groundbreaking; Division I athletics transition announcement; telemedicine program; nursing school gift announcement; Reservation for College inaugural scholarships celebration).

United States Coast Guard, *Report of Investigation into the Circumstances Surrounding the Incident Involving MC00004262-Polis' VSL CF3006KQ on 3/27/2000* (MISLE Activity Number: 87702; Originating Unit: MSO San Diego; MISLE Activity Owner: Commandant (G-MRI); MISLE Activity Controller: Commandant (G-MRI); MISLE Case Number: 82881).

University of California, *A Declaration of Community: Report of the Universitywide Campus Community Task Force*, 1993 (Dennis J. Galligani, Task Force Chair).

University of California, Davis, Division of the Academic Senate, *Bylaws of the Davis Division of the Academic Senate*, http://academicsenate.ucdavis.edu/bylaws_and_regulations/bylaws.cfm.

University of California, Davis, Emeriti Association Video Records Project, #43, *An Interview of Elmer Learn by James H. Meyer*, November 8, 1995.

University of California, Davis, Emeriti Association Video Records Project, #310, *An Interview of Robert E. Chason by Joe P. Tupin*, March 22, 2007.

University of California, Davis, Emeriti Association Video Records Project, #392, *An Interview of Frank J. Loge by Hibbard E. Williams*, September 4, 2013.

University of California, Davis, *Intercollegiate Athletics at UC Davis: A Student-Centered, Academically Focused Program, Report of the Academic Senate Special Committee on Athletics*, March 1, 2012 (Joe Kiskis, Committee Chair).

University of California, Davis, Iran Delegation News Conference, May 3, 2004, DVD.

University of California, Davis, *Summary Report of the Recruitment Advisory Committee for Director of Athletics*, December 2011 (Fred Wood, Committee Chair).

University of California, Davis, University Outreach and International Programs, "Building Bridges in the Middle East" DVD, 2007.

University of California, Davis, University Outreach and International Programs, "Rebuilding Bridges Between UC Davis and the Middle East, 1999-2009" DVD, 2009.

University of California, Davis, videotapes (Baja boating accident airport news conference, Freeborn memorial service, and Arboretum tree planting; Center for the Arts milestones; Mondavi Center opening night; Centennial Convocation).

University Woman: The Memoir of Celeste Turner Wright, Professor of English Emeritus; prefaces by J. Richard Blanchard and Robert A. Wiggins; interviews by A.I. Dickman and Robert A. Wiggins (Berkeley, CA: Regents of the University of California, 1981).

Amy Wallace, "End Race-Based Admissions, UC Regent Suggests" (*Los Angeles Times*, Jan. 20, 1995).

The Washington Post, "Outgoing UNC Chancellor Says College Presidents Need to Get Out of the Sports Business," June 5, 2013.

Susan J. Willoughby, *The Art Collection of UC Davis Health System* (Sacramento, CA: Fruitridge Printing, 2012).

Jafar Yaghoobi, *Let Us Water the Flowers: The Memoir of a Political Prisoner in Iran* (Amherst, NY: Prometheus Books, 2011).

ACKNOWLEDGMENTS

I'm particularly grateful for the assistance of two special colleagues—Cindy Geronimo Contreras and Maril Revette Stratton—in the production of this book.

For 25 years, Cindy has organized my work life, smoothing my way and my day while juggling competing demands in the hectic work environment of the Chancellor's Office. She brought her signature professionalism and focused efficiency to this project, as well. Her contributions were immense—from chasing down documents to verifying dates and details of long-ago calendared meetings, securing photos and videos, and exploring and mastering the particulars of digital book production. And I've just scratched the surface

Maril and I arrived at UC Davis just two years apart in the mid-1980s, so she experienced much of what I write about—initially from the vantage point of the campus's communications office (which she headed) and then from the Chancellor's Office (as associate chancellor/chief of staff), where her wisdom, perceptiveness and hard work helped make me a better chancellor. Her good memory, her good files and her familiarity with how I think, talk and feel made her the perfect book editing partner.

Midway through the book's production, our gifted graphic designer, Jan Conroy, tragically died in a car accident. He'd been delighted to join our book team. And we were thrilled to have him—an alum and new UC Davis retiree whose indelible graphic imprint had marked significant events in the life of the campus he'd loved and served for 35 years. I'm comforted knowing that this book will be yet another addition to his substantial legacy.

Jan's long-time and newly retired design colleague Laurie Lewis fittingly stepped in to pick up where Jan left off—not unlike how they'd passed work back and forth across 25 years as design colleagues. Together they'd created the foundation for the university's visual identity. And together they've helped me to present these stories—stories, Laurie says, that feel like hers, too. Her UC Davis roots go back the furthest of all of ours, clear back to the university's earliest days.

I'm indebted to Alumni Relations Assistant Vice Chancellor Richard Engel and to the Cal Aggie Alumni Association board for its support as I set out on my book venture. That early encouragement got the book-writing ball rolling.

So, too, am I appreciative of the early book-writing wisdom shared by Patricia Pelfrey, currently a research associate at UC Berkeley's Center for Studies in Higher Education.

She's a veteran UC book writer (her most recent is *Entrepreneurial President: Richard Atkinson and the University of California, 1995-2003*) and was generous with her time and knowledge.

As we explored digital publication possibilities—which gave us the opportunity to add audio and video to the book's text—we were immensely helped by these folks from UC's California Digital Library: Catherine Mitchell, Katrina Romanowsky, Katie Fortney, Lisa Schiff and Justin Gonder.

Finding and obtaining photographs proved much more challenging than we'd anticipated. Very special thanks are owed to Neil Michel of Axiom Photography and to Debbie Davis and Sue Cockrell of *The Davis Enterprise*, who always responded quickly and positively to each request.

Paul Ver Wey of Academic Technology Services was extraordinarily helpful in locating, editing and converting videos to the appropriate format for the digital version of *Indelibly Davis*. In the process, we learned how he has safeguarded a treasure trove of videos that would otherwise have been discarded. Instead, thanks to him, they are headed to our Library's Special Collections.

Many others generously shared their insights and memories or helped with our research: Martha Alcott, Vikram Amar, Gina Anderson, Steve Arditti, Patricia Bailey, Jodi Barnhill, Nicole Woolsey Biggart, Anne Bishop, Michael Boyd, Bob Brewer, Maureen Brodie, Gillian Butler, Lesley Byrns, Griselda Castro, Robert Chason, Jan Conroy, Gayle Dax-Conroy, Joyce Donaldson, Steven Drown, Thomas Dutton, Kimberly Elsbach, Sid England, Thomas Estes, Linda Fairfield, Craig Farris, Robert Franks, Lori Fulton, Jeremy Ganter, Kathy Keatley Garvey, Andrea Gaytan, Pam Gill-Fisher, Robert Grey, Jerry Hallee, Janet Hamilton, Geneva Harris, Sally Harvey, Becky Heard, Lorena Herrig, D. Kern Holoman, Irene Horgan-Thompson, Darlene Hunter, Bonnie Hyatt, Harold Hyde, Donna Justice, Rob Kerner, Robert Kerr, William Lacy, Kimberly Lane, Lisa Lapin, Lina Layiktez, John Lescroart, Laurie Lewis, Robert Loessberg-Zahl, Frank Loge, Rita Mae Lundin, James MacDonald, Judith Mack, Yvonne Marsh, Tammy McNiff, Linda Mijangos, Maureen Miller, Mohammad Mohanna, Margrit Mondavi, Jared Moses, Grant Nejedlo, Christine O'Dell, Christopher Ott, Patricia Pelfrey, Dolores Pence, Rex Perschbacher, Paul Pfotenhauer, Warren Pickett, Claire Pomeroy, Kimberly Pulliam, Kelly Ratliff, Rahim Reed, Nona Richardson, Pilar Rivera, Carol Robinson, Teri Robinson, Mike Robles, Bonnie Russell, Robert Segar, Nancy Sheehan, Dennis Shimek, Joseph Silva, John Skarstad, Sally Springer, Margaret Steward, Angela Taggart, Abigail Tilden, Dann Trask, Terry Tumey, Joe Tupin, Louise Uota, Neal Van Alfen, Rosalie Vanderhoef, Mikael Villalobos, John Vohs, Richard Vorpe, Pamela Walker, Carol Wall, Greg Warzecka, Nicole Waterman, Emmy Werner, Jean Wigglesworth, Hibbard Williams, Bruce Wolk, Trina Wood, Sylvia Wright and Wesley Young.

And several others readily pitched in when we needed their expertise and project help: Marjorie Ahl, Debbie Aldridge, Sue Barnes, Mitchel Benson, Janelle Bitker, Jan

Carmikle, Bella Corbin, Parvin Damania, Kathy Keatley Garvey, Karin Higgins, Kerie Holck, Kathleen Holder, Dave Jones, Jean Korinke, Jay Leek, Angela Malloy, Stephen McKone, Brian Nguyen, Erin Palmer, Ellen Pontac, Amanda Price, Carmen Raycraft, Mabel Salon, Russ Thebaud, Kit Tyler, Gregory Urquiaga, TJ Ushing, Jennifer Nicole-Wong Wade, Lisa Wade Wells, Mary Wood and Ken Zukin.

I'm so fortunate to have had their collective help.

Finally, I want to thank our UC Davis family—our faculty, staff, students, alumni and friends—for giving shape to our campus's rich narrative. Share your stories. Write new ones. And keep alive that special Davis spirit that first sparked more than a century ago.

INDELIBLY DAVIS

About the Author

LARRY N. VANDERHOEF is chancellor emeritus and distinguished professor emeritus at the University of California, Davis.

The first in his family to complete high school, and one of the very few in his Wisconsin foundry town to make his way to college, he became one of the nation's longest-serving university leaders and is widely credited with mentoring future university presidents and provosts.

A plant biologist turned college administrator, he led UC Davis for 25 years—first as provost/executive vice chancellor (1984-94) and then as chancellor (1994-2009).

Under his leadership, the campus grew by nearly every measure: student population, faculty, rankings, facilities, stature, research funding and philanthropic donations (including the launch of UC Davis' first comprehensive campaign, with nearly half of its $1 billion goal raised by the time he stepped down as chancellor).

Vanderhoef made good on an inaugural promise to build a world-class performing arts center at UC Davis—just one of numerous state-of-the-art facilities constructed on his watch—and led the university itself to a more prominent place on the world stage.

Overcoming his Midwestern reserve, he became an outspoken advocate for access to higher education and an academic diplomat—working throughout his tenure to "build bridges" to schools in inner-city Sacramento as well as universities in countries such as Iran.

In leading UC Davis through state budget cuts, the aftermath of campus and national tragedies and other challenges, Vanderhoef developed a reputation for being a principled, approachable leader. He was willing to make tough decisions, and remains passionate about the university's mission to make people's lives better.

His research interests lie in the general area of plant growth and development, and in the evolution of the land-grant universities. He has taught classes from freshman level to advanced graduate study, and has served on various national commissions addressing graduate and international education, the role of a modern land-grant university and accrediting issues.

Previously, he held faculty and administrative positions at the University of Illinois and at the University of Maryland, College Park. Early in his career, he was named an Eisenhower Fellow, a recognition awarded to emerging leaders from around the world to promote positive relationships and interactions between countries.

Vanderhoef is a fellow of the American Association for the Advancement of Science and of the American Society of Plant Biologists. He received B.S. and M.S. degrees from the University of Wisconsin, Milwaukee, and a Ph.D. from Purdue University, as well as honorary doctoral degrees from Purdue University and Inje University in Korea and an honorary professorship from China Agricultural University.

As chancellor emeritus, he continues to serve on multiple university and regional advisory boards, developed and taught an undergraduate biology course at UC Davis and at National Taiwan University and National Chung Hsing University, served on the U.S. Department of Education's National Advisory Committee on Institutional Quality and Integrity, and chaired the California Public Utilities Commission's Independent Review Panel investigating the 2010 San Bruno Gas Explosion.

About UC Davis

The University of California, Davis, is one of 10 UC campuses and one of a select group of 62 North American universities admitted to membership in the prestigious Association of American Universities.

UC Davis has earned a stellar reputation for outstanding faculty and students, a distinguishing breadth of academic programs and dedication to interdisciplinary study, global leadership in sustainability, and a commitment to addressing society's needs through innovative research and public service.

Located near the California state capital, UC Davis has more than 35,000 students, the full-time equivalent of 4,100 faculty and other academics and 17,400 staff, an annual research budget of more than $750 million, about two dozen specialized research centers, a veterinary medical teaching hospital, and a comprehensive health system that includes an acute-care hospital in Sacramento and a multi-specialty physician group serving 33 counties and six million residents. The university offers interdisciplinary graduate study and 102 undergraduate majors in four colleges—Agricultural and Environmental Sciences, Biological Sciences, Engineering, and Letters and Science—and six professional schools—Education, Law, Management, Medicine, Veterinary Medicine and the Betty Irene Moore School of Nursing.

A birds-eye view of the bike circle by the Quad. (Photo: UC Davis/Karin Higgins)